I Affectionately Dedicate This Book

to

My Wife

In Token Of Her Valuable Assistance

Contents

ADVENTURE

ADVENTURE

Introduction

When I was a boy I was always eager to know the "why" and "how" of things. I was forever wanting to know how things were made and what made them go. Like other boys I, too, took clocks apart and, like other boys, I, too, failed to put them together again. But since they were old clocks, no harm was done and I learned something of how they were put together and I had a lot of fun doing it.

Now that you are about to use a microscope, I think that you should know something about such an instrument before beginning to work with it. But before I tell you about the different parts, perhaps you would first like to know how the microscope came to be invented.

To begin with, lenses, for the purpose of magnifying objects, were first used as early as the thirteenth century. We know this from recorded history but it is quite possible that they may have been used even earlier, for I believe you will agree with me that the ancient gem-cutters could hardly have accomplished their work without some artificial aid. Of course, they may have used spheres of glass filled with water as magnifiers, since such magnifiers were known at least as early as 63 A.D. In that year the Roman historian, Seneca, wrote that "letters, though small and dim, are seen enlarged and more distinct through a glass globe filled with water." The ancients, not as quick-witted as we are in this enlightened age, failed, however, to recognize the practical implications of such a phenomenon as an aid to vision, for the medical writers up to the thirteenth century repeatedly speak of short-sightedness as an incurable ailment.

In the eleventh century an Arabian physician by the name of Alhagen seems to have had the germ of an idea, for in a publication presumed to date from about 1052, he describes the use of lenses for producing enlarged images. Two centuries later, Roger Bacon, the English monk, noted the same effect, but that is as far as he got. Later in the same century, that is, the thirteenth, along came a Florentine, name of Salvino d'Armato degli Armati, who really did something by taking lenses and putting them in a frame to relieve defects of vision. So with Edison, Bell, Fulton, and all the other great inventors, we can place Salvino as the inventor of spectacles.

Now what puzzles me is why lenses were not used at that time for examining objects too minute to be studied with the unaided eye. But about three hundred years passed before scientists discovered that they could use lenses in studying the minute structures of natural objects. Then, as if to make up for lost time, they vied with one another in looking at things. Sooner or later it had to come, and at last, in 1637, the French philosopher and physicist Descartes published a diagram of a microscope. This diagram shows us an instrument containing a single lens in which rays of light were reflected onto the object by means of a concave mirror. A few years later, in 1665, an Englishman, Richard Hooke, used small glass balls, formed by fusing threads of drawn glass in place of convex lenses. These were set in metal plates, the object to be examined being mounted on some sort of movable arm.

So far so good. But the scientists of that time had just begun to get busy. They were not satisfied with merely using one lens, so they tried using two at a time. This idea seems to have first been conceived by Leonard Digges, also an Englishman. But he doesn't appear to have done much with it and it remained for a pair of Dutch spectacle makers, Hans and Zacharias Janssen, to make the first practical instrument. This was in 1590, and it is to them that the invention of the compound microscope is attributed. The Italians, however, not satisfied with having the invention of spectacles to their credit, also wanted to take credit for the invention of the compound microscope, for the famous Italian astronomer Galileo also invented such an instrument in 1610. To me, it seems that their claim was a trifle belated.

These early compound microscopes and their illuminating apparatus were cumbrous and unwieldy and really had little practical importance because of complications introduced by spherical and chromatic aberration, which we do not need to go into. It is enough to say that for two centuries they were inferior to the best simple microscope. But such is the ingenuity of man that finally, between 1820 and 1830, the difficulties caused by spherical and chromatic aberration were overcome, and from that time on, the compound microscope acquired a new importance and gradually developed into one of the most important instruments of modern science.

The compound microscope, as distinguished from the simple, contains two or more lenses or systems of lenses, one of which forms an image of the object, while the other forms a second image of the first. One of the lenses is called an objective lens, or simply objective, and is so called because the rays of light from the object first pass through it. The objective is mounted in a tube, the purpose of which is to exclude from the eye all rays of light except those passing through the objective from the object, and in the other end of this tube is mounted another and shorter tube in which is fixed the ocular or eyepiece through which the magnified image formed by the objective is further magnified and viewed by the eye. For steadiness, these optical parts are mounted upon a rigid stand, with an apparatus for throwing light upon the object to be examined and for focusing or so adjusting the relation between the object and the lenses that a clear image may be formed.

If the microscope which you possess happens to be a compound one, you can learn the names of the different parts by comparing it with Figure 1. If it is made in America it should have a base shaped like a horseshoe. From the base there rises a vertical pillar which is provided at its upper end with an inclination joint, and into which fits the lower part of the arm. By means of this inclination joint you can tilt the arm, and also

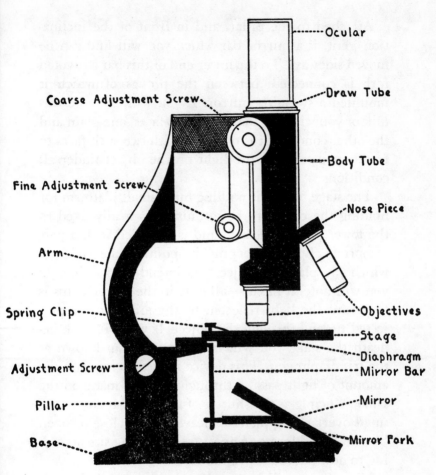

FIGURE 1

The Parts of a Microscope

the body of the instrument, to any angle between the vertical and horizontal, but you can keep it in such a position only by tightening one of the nuts which are threaded to both ends of a conical pin which runs through both the pillar and the arm.

Attached to the pillar, and in front of the inclination joint, is a mirror bar which you will find can be moved sideways. To the lower end of this bar a pivoted fork is connected, between the prongs of which is mounted a swinging mirror. If you will examine this mirror you will find that it has two faces, one plain and the other concave. It is provided with two such faces to enable you to focus the light on the object under all conditions.

The stage, which is nothing but a small platform for holding the object to be examined, is firmly fixed to the lower part of the arm and is provided with a pair of spring clips for keeping in position the slide on which you place the object you intend to examine. As you will note, it has a small hole in the center. This is to permit the light reflected by the mirror to be projected up and through the object. If you will look beneath the stage you will find a mechanism known as the iris diaphragm. This device is used to regulate the amount of light passing through it and is made on the same principle as the shutter of a camera. It consists of small overlapping plates or leaves which close or open by a lever and forms an aperture of varying size according to how far you move the lever.

Now if you will look at the upper part of the arm you will find another mechanism consisting of a rack, which is merely a strip of metal with teeth cut in it and fixed to the body tube, and a pinion, which is a small toothed wheel mounted on the arm. This mechanism is to enable you to focus rapidly on the object. The teeth of one mesh with the teeth of the other, and the rack is moved by turning the coarse adjustment screw.

The direction in which the screw is turned determines the up and down movement of the rack. In addition to the coarse adjustment, there is also a fine adjustment to enable you to focus more delicately on the object. This mechanism is regulated by turning the fine adjustment screw.

We next turn our attention to the body tube. This is attached to the rack and acts as a support for the lenses, though it carries no lenses itself. It is divided into two parts—the tube proper and an inner cylinder, called the draw-tube. This draw-tube may be withdrawn from its upper end, telescope fashion, and its purpose is to vary the distance between the ocular or eyepiece and the objective, thus increasing or decreasing the magnification of the object. Attached to the lower end of the body tube you will find a revolving element known as the nosepiece, into which are fitted the objectives. This device is so constructed as to permit you to change from one objective to another by merely turning the nosepiece around until the objective which you want is under the body tube and in line with the ocular or eyepiece, which is carried by the upper end of the draw-tube.

If you examine the ocular or eyepiece you will find stamped on it either a letter or a number. This letter or number indicates its magnification. For instance, if the ocular is marked 5X it means that the ocular magnifies 5 times. And if the objective has a magnifying power of 10X, in other words, if the image formed by it is ten times larger than the object itself, the virtual image produced by the ocular 5X will be 5 times as large as the image produced by the objective, or fifty times larger than the object itself. To find the magnification of an object then, you merely multiply the magnifying power of the objective by that of the ocular.

As the microscope is a delicate instrument that might easily be injured through carelessness or neglect, and I am sure that you do not want anything to happen to it, I shall give you a few simple rules which you would do well to observe at all times. In the first place, you should see to it that it is kept scrupulously clean, and when you are not using it you should keep it in its case or under a bell jar. If particles of dust settle upon it—and they are very apt to, no matter how careful you may be—you should remove them with a camel's hair brush or chamois skin. If any dust settles on the lenses, however, you should remove it with a piece of very soft linen or, better still, with a piece of Japanese lens paper. Never use a chamois skin on the lens, for it contains natural oils which are apt to form a film on the surface of the lens and thus cause dust and dirt to stick to it, which is just what you don't want to happen. Be sure when cleaning the lens that you rub gently, for the glass is easily scratched. Never touch the lens with your fingers, as they also contain natural oils and some perspiration, which is very difficult to remove. If for any reason you cannot clean the lens by merely wiping it, moisten the Japanese paper with a drop or two of alcohol or xylol, but be sure that you wipe the lens perfectly dry after using such cleansing agents.

Always handle the microscope by the base so as not to subject the mechanical parts to any undue strain.

When using it, you should place it rather near the edge of the table or workbench. You should sit close to the table in a chair that will bring your eyes a little above the level of the eyepiece. Most microscopists do not tilt the microscope but you may do so at times when examining dry objects. Obviously, you cannot do so when working with fresh mounts or fluids, for the stage will have to be kept parallel with the table top.

When using the microscope you must have the proper illumination if you want to obtain the best results. You should avoid direct sunlight, but you may use a clear area of sky, or you may use sunlight reflected from a white wall to advantage. If you have to use artificial illumination, you must use a light which does not flicker. An electric bulb with a ground glass shade may be used in such a case.

Ordinarily you will find that the flat surface of the mirror will give you sufficient light, but if you should need stronger illumination, then use the concave surface. In any event, you should always adjust the mirror in relation to the window or lamp so that a clear and well-defined circle of light may be seen.

When you have set the microscope up and have the field well lighted, the next step is to focus on the object, or to adjust the relation of the lenses so that a clear image may be formed. To do this, first bring the low objective down to within an eighth of an inch of the object or cover glass, using the coarse adjustment for the purpose. You should always use the low objective for a preliminary examination before a new specimen is examined with the higher powers, as it shows more of the object and gives you a better idea of its general appearance. While using the coarse adjustment, you should watch the movement of the objective from the side so as not to run it into the object, for should you do so you might damage the lens. Then, looking through the microscope, raise the objective slowly, again by using the coarse adjustment, until a point is reached when you may clearly see the object. When this point is reached, bring the fine adjustment into play, which will give you the sharpest focus possible and therefore the best definition. In using the fine adjustment, you will find that only a certain plane of the object will be in focus, while its whole figure is needed to make up a correct picture. Thus you should continually and slightly vary the fine adjustment as needs demand. Should you wish a greater magnification of the object, then swing the nosepiece around until the higher objective is in line with the ocular, and then focus with the fine adjustment.

As a final hint, in no case should you strain your eyes in an attempt to study what you cannot see clearly. If the object is not distinct, there is something wrong which should be remedied. You should learn to use both eyes alternately, and to acquire the habit of keeping open the eye which is not over the instrument. You may at first be distracted by external objects, but this difficulty will disappear with a little practice. You may also be misled by seeing through the microscope certain cloudy specks floating across the field of view. These are the *muscae volitantes,* shreds of matter lying in the vitreous humor of the eye, but after a while you will grow so accustomed to them that you will be unaware of their presence.

xx

And now that you have become familiar with the parts of a microscope and how to use it, I am quite sure that you will get many hours of fun and pleasure out of your instrument and from the adventures on which we are about to set out.

Useful Supplies for Your Laboratory Table and Shelf

APPARATUS—CHEMICAL REAGENTS AND STAINS

Microscope
Case or Bell Jar
Life Slides
Slides (Plain)
Watch Glass
Cover Glasses
Dipping Tube
Glass Rod
Wide Mouthed Bottle
Killing Jar
Flat Dish
Test Tube

Tweezers
Scissors
Fine-pointed Curved
   Forceps
Scalpel
Dissecting Needle
Knife
Razor Blade
Blotting Paper
Reading Lens
Small Brush
Camel's Hair Brush
Chamois Skin
Japanese Lense Paper

Acetic Acid
One Per Cent Chloretone
Methyl Green

Gelatine
Baking Soda
Methylene Blue

Chloroform
Glycerine
Eosin
Sodium Chloride (Salt)
Alcohol
Caustic Potash
Xylol
Limewater

Canada Balsam
Borax Carmine
Sulphuric Acid
Potassium Permanganate
Chlorinated Soda
Ether
Iodine
Vaseline

ADVENTURE 1

We Examine Some Common Objects

For our first adventure we shall examine a few simple and common objects in order to get the "feel" of the microscope and the "hang" of its use. I know of no object more common or more easily obtainable than a hair from one's own head. So we will proceed to pull one out and place it on a slide in a drop of water. Then

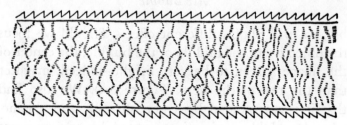

FIGURE 2

A Human Hair

cover it with a cover glass, which we handle by means of a pair of fine-pointed curved forceps. Transferring the slide to the stage of the microscope, we examine it. We find it appears as shown in Figure 2.

Having satisfied ourselves as to what a hair looks like, we next proceed to examine an air bubble. To obtain such a bubble, we place on a clean slide a small fragment of blotting paper, torn from a larger piece so that it will have rough frayed edges. We wet it with water, using a glass rod for the purpose. Small air bubbles will be entangled in the fibers of the paper. Then cover the whole with a clean cover glass. On viewing the air bubbles we shall find that they appear as dark spots with shining centers. If we focus to different parts of a bub-

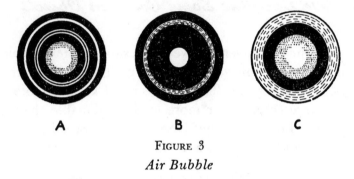

A   B   C

FIGURE 3

Air Bubble

ble, we will obtain different effects. Should we focus the objective to the middle of the bubble, the center of the image is seen to be very bright—indeed, brighter than the rest of the field (Figure 3A). We also find that it is surrounded by a grayish zone, and a somewhat broad black ring interrupted by one or more brighter circles, and that around the black ring are again one or more concentric circles brighter than the field.

If we focus to the bottom of the bubble we shall see that the central white circle diminishes and becomes brighter (Figure 3B), that its margin is sharper, and

FIGURE 4
Scale of a Herring

that it is surrounded by a very broad black ring which has on its periphery one or more diffraction circles.

And lastly, on focusing to the upper surface of the bubble, we shall note that the central circle increases in size, and is surrounded by a greater or lesser number of rings of various shades of gray, around which is a black ring but narrower than those that we found in the other two positions of the objective. (Figure 3C)

Fish scales are easily obtainable and also make beautiful objects for low powers. As they are often coated with a tenacious mucous material, this should first be removed by washing in a solution of caustic potash. The fish scales, like the piece of hair which we examined, should also be viewed in water. Figure 4 shows a scale from the herring.

Many of the smaller kinds of plant seeds are very curious-looking and some of them are extremely beautiful when

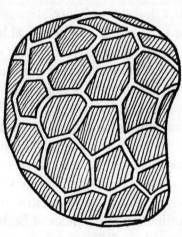

FIGURE 5
Poppy Seed

3

viewed with a low power. The seed of the poppy, for instance, will appear as having a number of hexagonal pits on its surface (Figure 5). That of the snapdragon is strangely irregular in shape, while that of the carrot reminds one of a starfish. As you examine others that may be handy you will observe that they all have more or less individual characteristics.

ADVENTURE 2

We Become Crystal Gazers

Do not let the heading of this adventure mislead you. We are not going to peer into such crystals as fortune tellers use, in which they claim to be able to predict that some rich relative is going to leave you money, or some equally nonsensical bosh. Our crystals are to be the tiny geometrical bodies of which many substances are composed. Little do you realize, perhaps, that as you dissolve a spoonful of sugar in your coffee or sprinkle some salt on your food, you unwittingly are destroying thousands of beautiful tiny gems.

Perhaps you already know that both of these substances exist in crystalline form. On the other hand, you may be a doubting Thomas, or, like the man from Missouri, you want to be shown. In either case, let us examine a few particles of both substances, as I am quite sure you will want to view some of the most beautiful objects to be seen with the microscope.

4

Now, if we look at sugar or salt as it comes from the grocery store, I am afraid we wouldn't see much worth looking at, and so it becomes necessary for us to prepare our crystals, which is a very easy thing to do. To obtain such crystals, we simply dissolve some sugar or salt in a little hot water until we find that the water will not dissolve any more. We then transfer a drop or two of each solution to a clean slide and wait until the excess water has evaporated. When most of the water seems to have disappeared, we transfer the slide to the stage of the microscope. If we examine the slide containing the salt crystals first, we shall find that we have a number of little crystal cubes. Perhaps we shall also find some crystals which have departed somewhat from the cubic form, the departure in such instances being due to impurities in the water or salt. If we used iodized salt we should also find some colored crystals of iodine. But if the salt is chemically pure we should see nothing but perfect cubes.

We next examine the sugar, but in this case we shall be less able to see any definite arrangement of the crystals, as sugar does not crystallize at once from a saturated solution in water. If we set the slide aside for a day or so the crystals will, at the end of that time, have formed.

Now, sugar and salt are not the only crystals we can obtain and examine; there is a vast number of others such as alum, borax, washing soda, potassium permanganate, iron sulphate and copper sulphate, to name but a few. These are all common and easily obtained, and are all soluble in water.

We can watch the crystals in the process of formation

if we want to. All that is necessary is to transfer the slide to the microscope when most of the water appears to have evaporated, for it is at this point that crystallization begins. I am sure that you will find it a most

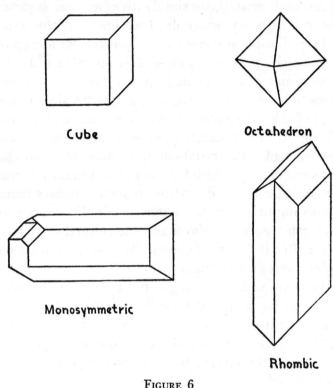

Cube

Octahedron

Monosymmetric

Rhombic

FIGURE 6
Crystals

interesting sight to see the first crystal take shape, to be followed by others, until there appears a number of these tiny glistening gems. Extremely beautiful crystals may be obtained from certain substances, such as potassium bichromate, for instance. Copper sulphate, if dissolved in gelatine, will form lovely fern-like crystals that for beauty will rival the ice crystals that form on window panes in extremely cold weather and which are so familiar to us. To dissolve the copper sulphate in gelatine, gently warm the gelatine to which is added an equal volume of water. When the gelatine has all dissolved, add the copper sulphate until the point is reached when no more will dissolve. Then proceed as before.

As you watch the crystal formation of various substances you will observe that the crystals assume a definite form, the form varying according to the substance used. The salt crystals, as we have seen, form a perfect cube. Alum, on the other hand, assumes the form of the octahedron, while potassium permanganate the rhombic form, and rock candy, which is pure sugar, the mono-symmetric form (Figure 6), names which may sound familiar to you, particularly if you have studied geometry.

ADVENTURE 3

We Hunt a One-Eyed Monster

Our third adventure takes us on the quest for a one-eyed monster. If you remember your Greek mythology, there existed at one time a race of one-eyed giants called Cyclops. Actually, of course, the Cyclops never existed and perhaps it was just as well, for if they had been anything like the one-eyed monsters to be found in the microscopic world, called Cyclops after their fabled prototypes, the world would indeed have been a terrifying place to live in. The Cyclops of which we speak are nothing but water fleas, and to us they do not look very big, but to the other animals that inhabit the microscopic world they appear no doubt as terrifying, ferocious ogres.

They live in ponds and spring pools and all we need in order to catch them is a wide-mouthed bottle. Armed with this, we make our way to the nearest pond or pool, and submerging the bottle in the water fill it almost to the top, being sure to gather up some of the mud and dead leaves, for it is among such things that the Cyclops hide. They are visible to the naked eye, and if we hold the bottle up to the light we should see them swimming about—little dots darting here and there, steadily and tirelessly.

But though we can see them with the naked eye, it is only under the microscope that we can see what they really look like. So we return home with our "catch" and set up our microscope. The next step is to transfer one of these one-eyed monsters from the bottle to a life slide * which we place on the stage of the microscope. For this purpose all we need is a dipping tube.** Placing the tip of the forefinger over the upper end, we dip the lower into the water and move it about until it is close to one of the Cyclops. Then we remove our finger, at which the water and Cyclops will rush up into

* A life slide is a slide with a small depression in it, and may be obtained from any supply house or dealer in microscopes.
** A dipping tube is merely a piece of glass tubing and may be obtained from any druggist.

the tube. Replacing the tip of the finger on the tube, we remove the tube. We find that the water and the imprisoned Cyclops will remain in the tube as long as we keep the finger on the upper opening. Placing the uncovered tip of the tube in the depression of the life slide, we remove the finger. Then the water will at once flow out, carrying Cyclops with it. By regulating the pressure through the movement of the finger, the water can be made to escape drop by drop, or in a sudden rush.

As Cyclops is a rather active little animal it may not remain quiet long enough for you to examine it properly. In that case you may quiet or anæsthetize it by placing in the depression of the life slide a solution of two parts of one per cent chloretone and five parts of water. You may also use this treatment for Daphnia which you will study in the next adventure.

We now have Cyclops where we want it, and so we adjust the microscope and examine it. As you will observe, it looks something like a miniature lobster (Figure 7). Indeed, it not only looks like a lobster but, as a matter of fact, it is related to the lobster and such other animals as the shrimps and crabs, all of which have a hard shelly coating and for that reason are grouped together under the name of Crustacea, which is from the Latin *crusta,* skin.

You can spend many pleasant moments studying Cyclops and watching it move about, which it does by means of specially designed swimming feet. But first of all can you find its solitary eye, which gives it its name? Look carefully at the head and you will see it as a dark spot. And do you, by any chance, find two pear-shaped masses attached to the body, one on each side of the tail-like appendage which extends out from the tip of the abdomen? If you do, then you have caught a female, for the masses are eggs. In time the

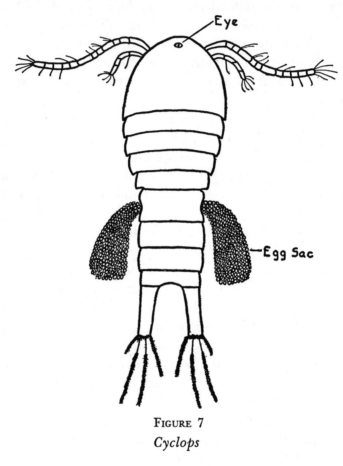

FIGURE 7
Cyclops

eggs will hatch, and if you can manage to keep them alive you will soon have a whole family of these little one-eyed monsters.

But here I must add a note of warning lest you think, when you see the young swimming about, that you have come across some other species of animal, for when the young Cyclops (Figure 8) hatch they do not look anything like their mother. It is only after they

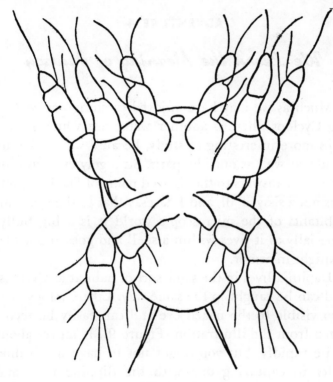

FIGURE 8
Young Form of Cyclops

have changed their skin several times that they begin to resemble their parent. So do not be fooled into thinking that the young Cyclops are entirely different

11

animals, which is exactly what they were believed to be until they were seen leaving their eggs. Then their true character was discovered.

We Learn the Meaning of Privacy

Much as we may have enjoyed catching and watching Cyclops, there is another water flea which is perhaps more interesting to study, because we can see its inside, as well as outside, parts. Strangely enough, this water flea answers to the sissified name of Daphnia, but it is not a sissy at all, and I daresay that to the other inhabitants of the microscopic world it is a big bully, especially as it lives within a shell and goes about like a knight in armor.

Daphnia lives in the same sort of habitat as Cyclops, and can be caught in the same way. Like Cyclops, it is also visible to the naked eye and can easily be recognized from the illustration (Figure 9). It moves about quite rapidly, but you ought not to have much difficulty in capturing one with the dipping tube and transferring it to the life slide. To be able to observe it at length it is necessary, however, to restrict its activity, and to keep it within range of the microscope, so do not give it too much water in which to swim about.

This little animal is a veritable dynamo, for if you watch it closely you will see that every part of it, both

12

inside and outside, appears to be moving. Do you notice its rapidly beating legs on the lower part of its body? But these are not legs at all, as we understand them. They are not used to walk or swim with, but to direct food into the animal's mouth as well as a stream

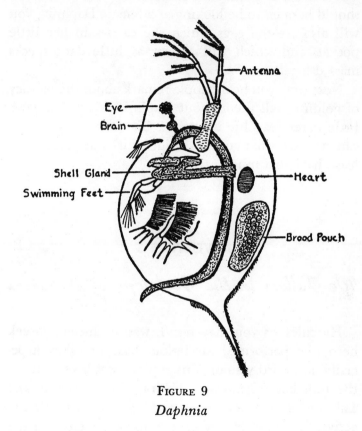

FIGURE 9
Daphnia

of water which contains a certain amount of dissolved oxygen without which it could not live.

Perhaps you do not realize what a wonderful sight you are witnessing. But you will when I point out that

13

here you have a complete view of a fairly complicated organic machine in operation. If you study Daphnia carefully you can see the passage of food through the alimentary tract, the blood flowing through the body, and even the contractions of the heart. And if you should happen to be looking at a female Daphnia, you will also see the eggs which she carries in her little pocket, and which will appear as little dark specks massed together.

Next time you hear people remark about the privacy of goldfish, tell them about Daphnia. Why, this poor little water flea's life is just one big open book, for we can even see what goes on inside of it. The goldfish, at least, have that much privacy.

We Follow in the Footsteps of Hercules

Hercules, as you may recall, was an ancient Greek hero who performed prodigious feats of valor. Especially noteworthy among his exploits was his slaying of the nine-headed monster Hydra which lived in the Lake of Lerna, where it was making itself unpleasantly active. Now we do not profess to be a hero like the mythological Hercules, but we shall try to follow in his footsteps and also hunt the Hydra, but with a different purpose.

Our Hydra, of course, is not a monster like the one

that terrified the inhabitants of ancient Greece, but a little fresh-water animal which we will find attached to the stems and leaves of underwater plants.

Although it is only under the microscope that we can really watch its activities, it can readily be seen with the naked eye. It looks much like a short, thick thread unraveled at one end. It is abundant in ponds and streams, where it may be found attached by one end to aquatic vegetation, especially to the rootlets of the small floating plants known as Duckweed.

As you will find when you examine it under the microscope (Figure 10), Hydra is really a hollow tube, attached by a basal disc at one end and with a mouth opening at the other, around which are arranged six to ten smaller tubes called tentacles. The entire animal is elastic, and, anchored to some aquatic plant, or other submerged object, it contracts and expands its body at will, meanwhile weaving its tentacles about in search of food. And woe to any victim that comes within their reach, for the tentacles, like those of the jelly-fish, are provided with stinging cells which

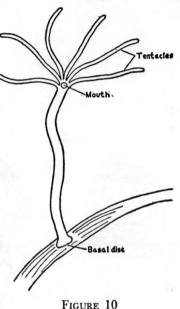

FIGURE 10
Hydra

15

shoot poisonous barbs into the delicate flesh of the prey.

These stinging cells, or nematocysts as they are called, located not only on the tentacles but all over the body, are small oval or pear-shaped bodies con-

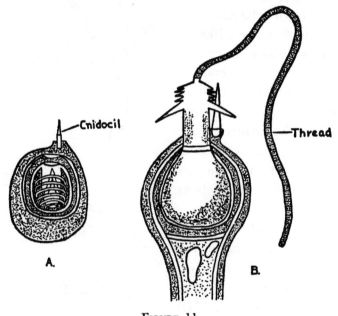

FIGURE 11
Nematocyst

A. Before discharge
B. After discharge

taining inverted, coiled, thread-like tubes with barbs at the base end and are brought into action by a trigger-like process, the cnidocil. When the nematocyst explodes, the tube turns rapidly inside out and is ejected with such force as to be able to penetrate the tissues of

16

other animals. Figure 11 shows a nematocyst before and after discharge. By applying a little acetic acid or methyl green you can get the Hydra to shoot off these stings. Then the threadlike tubes can be well seen.

Hydra lives on small aquatic animals, such as worms, which are seized by the tentacles as they swim by and conveyed to the mouth by the bending of the tentacle which effected the capture, although the other tentacles also assist in the operation. The mouth meanwhile opens and slowly moves around the food. This is then forced down into the body of the animal which serves as the stomach. There it is digested. If you want to see just how Hydra feeds, you might try feeding it small aquatic worms or if these are not handy, small bits of raw beefsteak. Be sure that the bits are small enough, and do not be discouraged if you don't succeed in getting it to eat at first—it may be that it is not hungry.

Hydra is not a stationary animal as you may think, but moves about from place to place much after the fashion of the measuring worm, though sometimes it uses its tentacles as legs or merely glides along on its basal disc.

If you should perchance come across a Hydra that looks as if it were a Siamese twin, you will have a Hydra reproducing. The process by which it reproduces is known as budding, and begins as a slight bulge or protuberance on the body wall. The bud, once started, pushes out rapidly into a stalk which soon develops a circlet of tentacles at its free end. The body of the young Hydra is hollow, and communicates with the body-cavity of the parent. It captures food like its parent, and sometimes both may be seen seizing the same prey. When full grown, the bud becomes detached and lives a free existence. Sometimes before the bud has become full grown it may begin to form other buds, the result being a sort of colony.

A very interesting characteristic of Hydra is its ability to regenerate or restore lost parts. Away back in 1744, a Dutch naturalist by the name of Trembly discovered that if the Hydra were cut into two, three or four pieces, each part would grow into an entire animal. He also found that when the head end is split in two and the parts separated slightly, a two-headed animal results. Parts of one Hydra may also easily be grafted upon another, and in this way many bizarre effects have been obtained.

ADVENTURE 6

We Learn How a Fly Walks Upside Down

During the course of our daily lives, we frequently meet with something that arouses our curiosity. But usually we are too busy or, to put it more bluntly, perhaps too lazy, to satisfy that curiosity. Take the ordinary house fly for instance. You have often seen it walk along the ceiling or perhaps up a window pane, and if your mental processes function normally, as I believe they do, no doubt you wondered how it manages to walk along such surfaces. But I daresay that is all you did about it. And that being the case suppose we now find out.

Our first step is to procure a fly. This should not be difficult in summer, for flies are only too common. There are many different species of flies but the one we are interested in is the common house fly which goes by the name of Musca. Now let us not go after Musca with a newspaper, for such a weapon would render our specimen unfit for our purpose. We must, on the contrary, capture and kill it in a manner that will not injure it, and to this end we make use of a killing jar such as entomologists use. Such a jar can be purchased from almost any scientific supply house for a nominal sum, but a homemade one, consisting of a wide-mouthed stoppered bottle containing a bit of cotton soaked in chloroform, will serve just as well.

To capture a house fly all you need to do is to approach your intended victim as stealthily as possible, and when the moment seems opportune place the uncovered bottle quickly over it. The best place to effect the capture is on a flat surface, for then there is no possible avenue of escape. The fly will search for one, however, and in doing so will fly up into the bottle. Then you should quickly replace the stopper.

When our victim has taken in enough of the poisonous fumes and shows no further signs of life, we remove it from the lethal chamber and proceed to remove one of its legs. This operation is not performed by merely pulling it off, as we may break it off in the wrong place, but by holding it in our tweezers with one hand while with the other we snip it off with a small pair of scissors, at the point where it is attached to the body.

Placing the severed leg on a slide, we transfer it to the stage of the microscope and proceed with our examination. To our astonishment, we find that the leg is thickly covered with hairs. Now we know that flies are carriers of disease, and it is in such hairy growth that they carry the destructive micro-organisms which are sometimes so fatal to human life. Moving the slide across our field of vision, we move it in the direction that will bring beneath the objective that end of the leg which is opposite to the end which was attached to the body. Here we find a pair of claws, and between these claws a little pad called the pulvillus (Figure 12). This pad contains glandular hairs which emit a transparent sticky fluid through minute pores, which permits the fly to walk on a smooth surface or upside down.

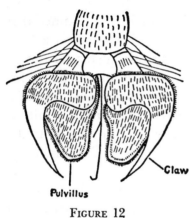

Claw

Pulvillus

FIGURE 12

A House Fly's Foot

Since we have our instruments at hand and a specimen for the purpose, let us examine other parts of the fly's anatomy. In the same manner as we severed the leg from the body, we cut off a wing. We examine it and find it to be rather a lace-like structure (Figure 13). The lines which you see are veins and divide the wing into spaces or cells. The distribution of these veins is of great importance to entomologists, for they are used in the classification of insects.

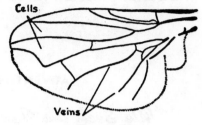

FIGURE 13
House Fly's Wing

As you will no doubt have observed when amputating the wing, the house fly has but one pair of wings, in contrast to other winged insects which have two pairs. In place of the hind wings, the fly has a pair of clubbed threads, known as halteres, which are supposed to be organs of equilibrium, for when one or both of them are removed the fly can no longer maintain its balance. Can you find them?

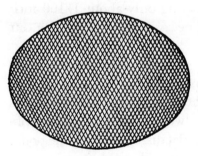

FIGURE 14
Eye of House Fly

Having satisfied our interest in the wing, we next remove an eye. This is a more delicate operation and involves the use of a scalpel. On viewing it through the microscope we find that it looks like a miniature golf ball (Figure 14.). Superficially it is divided into minute areas or facets which are more or less hexagonal as the result of mutual pressure. And you can believe it or not, but, there are supposed to be 4000 of them in the eye, so that we might say that

Musca has 8000 eyes in all. Is it any wonder, then, that it can see us from almost any angle, and so elude us with a facility that is often exasperating?

ADVENTURE 7

We Seek the Famous Amoeba

Of all the strange and queer animals to be found in the microscopic world, the oddest is, perhaps, the famous Amœba—an animal that has neither eyes, mouth or stomach. It is quite common and can be found in almost any shallow pool or pond where it lives among the aquatic plants. It is, however, too small to be seen with the naked eye, measuring only about 1/100 inch in diameter, so we find it necessary to seek it with our microscope.

Instead of taking home a jar of pond water and examining it drop by drop, a long and tedious process at best, the best way of obtaining one of these animals is to collect a mass of pondweed, preferably Ceratophyllum, which we place in a flat dish. Covering the pondweed with water, we next place the dish in a location where direct sunlight will not strike it, and let it stand until a brown scum appears on the surface of the water. This brown scum should contain a number of Amœbae and with a dipping tube we transfer some of it to a slide and examine it through our microscope.

The Amœba will be seen as an irregular colorless

particle of animated jelly (Figure 15), very soft and changeable in shape, slowly moving forward and suddenly altering its course and extending itself by protruding long blunt, finger-like projections of its own substance from any part of its body, which are lengthened or shortened at will, or withdrawn again into its

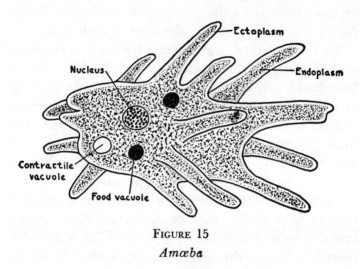

FIGURE 15
Amœba

own substance, where they entirely disappear. Looking at it closely you will see that it is made up of two regions—an outer colorless region free of granules called the ectoplasm and an inner granular region called the endoplasm. In the endoplasm you may or may not see, depending on the conditions, a fairly large roundish structure, called the nucleus, a body which is necessary to the life of the animal, for if an Amœba is cut in two the part containing the nucleus lives while the other part dies.

You may also be able to see a clear space filled with

a fluid less dense than the surrounding medium. This is the contractile vacuole, so called from the fact that its walls contract at more or less regular intervals; and its function is to get rid of the water taken in through the surface of the body. There is also a third structure which is but temporary in character. This is the food vacuole, formed by the particles of food eaten by the Amœba. It is used for the digestion of such food.

Speaking of food, the Amœba feeds on microscopic animal and vegetable matter, but if it has no mouth how does it eat, you ask? We can best explain this necessary performance by means of a simple experiment. Take a small solid particle—a pea for instance—and some glycerine or white of egg and let it flow about and around the pea. Pretty soon you will find that the gylcerine or white of egg will completely have engulfed the pea. The Amœba feeds in like manner and may take in food on any part of its body. Let us assume that the Amœba is in search of food. When a desirable morsel is found, the finger-like projection which located it begins to expand and a wave of the body substance flows along it until the object is entirely surrounded, when the finger-like projection will be withdrawn into the body, carrying the food with it. Food may be taken in at any point on the surface of the body, but it is usually taken in at what may be called the temporary anterior end, that is, the part of the body toward the direction of locomotion.

The food which the Amœba eats does not go into a stomach, for the animal has none. Instead it forms a food vacuole—a structure whose contents consists of the food particles suspended in water, which was taken in at the same time as the food. As soon as this vacuole has been formed, a secretion of some mineral acid then enters through the walls of the vacuole and proceeds to dissolve the food substances contained within it. All undigested particles are egested at any point on the surface of the animal, for there is no special opening to the exterior for the waste material. As a rule, such particles are heavier than the substance of the animal, and, as the Amœba moves forward, they fall behind, eventually passing out at the end away from the direction of movement.

The food which the Amœba eats goes into the making of energy for its various physical activities. If more food is eaten than is thus used up, this is added to the substance of the animal, the result being an increase in size. This is growth as we understand it. Now as we grow to a certain size and then stop, so likewise does the Amœba. When this certain size is reached, which rarely exceeds 1/100 inch in diameter, a strange thing happens: the animal divides in two, and in place of one Amœba there are now two, both of which take up a separate existence.

As you watch the Amœba move about, you will note that it does so by means of finger-like projections of the body, known as pseudopodia or false legs. As a rule it moves rather slowly, but sometimes the movements are active, the Amœba extending its pseudopodia and then gliding along as though its body were formed of the white of an egg. One can never predict what direction the Amœba may take at a moment's notice. The front may, without any warning at all, suddenly become the rear, or pseudopodia may be extended from some other portion of the body, those in front meanwhile being withdrawn into the substance and disappearing as it follows some other course.

The Amœba is one of the simplest animals, yet it exhibits all of the essential biological characteristics attributed to the most complex animals. It has no mouth, yet it can eat; it has no stomach, yet it can digest food; it has no eyes, yet it can direct or alter its course when obstacles lie in its way; and it has no nerves, yet when disturbed it can contract into a small ball-like mass. The Amœba is, thus, not only an interesting animal to watch but also to study, as it gives us an understanding of the life processes which go on in all living things, from the lowest, simplest animals to the highest, including ourselves.

ADVENTURE 8

We Meet with a Puzzle of Natural History

While searching for the Amœba, in the culture which you prepared for our last adventure, did you by any chance come across a minute, somewhat elongated creature with a long whip-like process attached to one end, as pictured in Figure 16? This creature, known as Euglena, has long been the subject of dispute between zoologists and botanists, and recalls to our mind Hamlet's famous soliloquy, "To be or not to be," for the zoologists claim it to be an animal, while the botanists hold that it is a plant.

Now there is something to be said for both sides. The zoologists point out that it exhibits a number of animal characteristics, one of which is its ability to move about freely, swimming by means of the whip-like process which is called a flagellum. On the other hand, the botanists argue that it does not eat, like other animals, ready-made food, but, like plants, manufactures its own food, doing so by means of a green coloring matter called chlorophyll which, as in plants, is able in the presence of light to break down carbon dioxide, thus setting free the oxygen

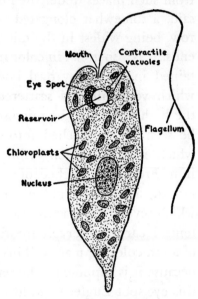

FIGURE 16

Euglena

and to unite the carbon with water, forming a substance somewhat similar to starch. Without going into other plant and animal characteristics, it would seem rather obvious that it is neither wholly plant nor wholly animal, but part plant and part animal. There are some three hundred more of such plant-animals and collectively they represent a group called the Flagellates, which is neither plant nor animal, but intermediate, forming a bridge, as it were, between the two kingdoms.

Euglena, which is a typical form of this group, lives in small bodies of fresh water, and as it is rather common it can usually be obtained by examining material from such places under the microscope. It is, as I have said, a somewhat elongated creature, and rather narrow, being widest in the middle and tapering to both ends. It is also green in color from the chlorophyll contained in the many oval bodies, called chloroplasts, which you will find scattered throughout it. Under the high power of the microscope, the front end may be seen to be notched into a sort of opening from which extends the long vibrating and colorless flagellum. From the notched opening, which is called the mouth, a tubular "gullet" leads to a reservoir, into which several contractile vacuoles discharge their contents. Near the reservoir are what appear to be granules of a red coloring matter. This is the eye-spot, so called because it is supposed to be sensitive to light. Without this eye-spot Euglena would find itself in a sorry state indeed, for since, as we have seen, it manufactures its own food and needs sunlight to do so, it must have some means of locating such an essential agency. Nature has therefore made Euglena very sensitive to light and we accordingly find that it ordinarily swims toward light. Proof of this can be easily obtained by merely examining a culture containing Euglenæ, when most of the animals will be found to be on the brightest side.

Euglena reproduces by dividing down the middle, the division beginning at the anterior end, that is, the end where the flagellum is attached. The old flagellum is retained by one half, while a new one is developed by the other. In the autumn it forms a thick-walled resting spore—a plant characteristic, by the way—which lasts over winter and germinates in the spring, each spore producing four new plant-animals.

While the Flagellates are typically single individuals, they frequently form gelatinous colonies, which are either globular and free floating or attached and variously branched. One of such floating

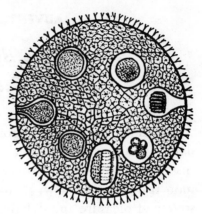

FIGURE 17

Volvox

colonies is Volvox (Figure 17) which will appear as a small globe or sphere, spinning or rolling continuously through the water in a most graceful manner. Viewing it through the microscope we will find that it appears to be made up of spheres within spheres. These are the individual cells, and may number as many as twelve thousand. We shall also find that the outer surface is studded with flagella which vibrate continually, thus lashing the water and giving rise to the rolling motion. The deep-green balls which you may see within the larger globe are young plant-animals in various stages of development. When they become mature, the mother-globe is ruptured, and the young plant-animals then float out and roll away through the water to take up an independent existence.

ADVENTURE 9

We Dig for Bones in an Ancient Graveyard

Tooth-paste is a rather prosaic article and we use it daily without giving it much thought. But here is an instance of how we go through life passing by the common things we meet with, and little realizing what a source of pleasure and delight they could give us if we only stopped and became better acquainted with them. So it is with tooth-paste; not with every tooth-paste, I must admit, but those made of diatomaceous earth, of which I will say more later. And if I were to tell you that such a tooth-paste contained the most exquisite and marvelous lace-like little bodies with a penchant for variety and daintiness that passes description, you would not believe me. But smear a little of it on a slide and examine it through your microscope and you will see these little bodies for yourself.

What are they? They are the fossil skeletons of minute plants that lived millions of years ago. And unlike many things that lived so long ago and have since become extinct, these plants still live. As a matter of fact, they are very abundant and can be found in almost every pond or pool, yes, in almost every ditch or mud-hole for that matter. Singly they are invisible to the naked eye, but often they are found in large numbers, forming a yellowish-brown film on the surface of the water, when they may be skimmed up and so gathered. Otherwise they may be obtained by scraping up some of the mud or by collecting some of the larger water plants to which they are frequently attached.

These plants, known as Diatoms, are usually brown in color, from the mud in which they live, and aside from this characteristic they may be distinguished from other plants, which are generally green, by their peculiar structure. They have often been compared to a pill-box. As you will observe, each Diatom is formed

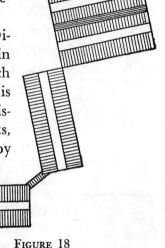

FIGURE 18

Diatoma

of two box-shaped parts, called valves, one of which may be likened to the pill-box proper and the other to the lid, as it overlaps or slips over the upright edge of the lower valve, much as the cover may slip over a paper box.

Another feature by which to distinguish the Diatoms is that they are all highly geometric in form—circles, ovals, triangles, and with patterns so precise that we might think they had been laid out with mechanical drawing instruments. Many of them are marked and regularly decorated with lines of partly raised ribs or tubercles and partly sunken pits, slits, or pores, making them some of the most beautiful things to be found in the microscopic world. Some two thousand species have been described, a few of which we show in Figures 18-19-20.

FIGURE 19
Encyonema

The walls of the Diatoms are densely infiltrated or impregnated with silica which makes their pill-box cases indestructable. Thus each Diatom lives in what may be termed a majestic sarcophagus, for the beautiful shells or skeletons persist long after the living part of the plant has died. As a result, beds, often of immense size, of such shells or skeletons may be found in many parts of the world. Such beds or "mud" of which many small lakes are filled, are composed, as a rule, chiefly of living Diatoms near the top, of their partially decayed remains lower down, and of their pure white empty shells at the bottom. Such deposits furnish a substance called "diatomaceous earth," which is used as a base for most polishing powders and tooth-

FIGURE 20
Pleurosigma

32

pastes, of which I have spoken, and to some extent for mixture with nitroglycerine in the manufacture of certain grades of dynamite.

ADVENTURE 10

We Make the Acquaintance of the Desmids

Similar in some ways to the Diatoms, but differing in others, is another group of microscopic plants called the Desmids. They also are found in fresh water, where they live mostly around the margins and bottoms of ponds, sometimes attached by a colorless jelly which they secrete from their walls. Like the Diatoms they too are, singly, invisible to the naked eye, but collectively they may be seen as a green film adhering to the stems of other plants.

You should have no

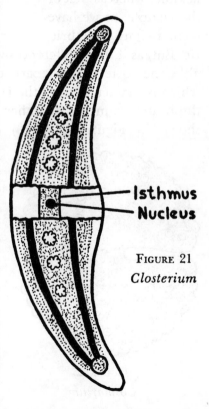

— Isthmus
— Nucleus

FIGURE 21
Closterium

trouble in distinguishing the Desmids from the Diatoms for, in the first place, they are green in color. In the second place, the wall of a Desmid—that is the thin envelope which surrounds the green contents — is soft and flexible, whereas that of the Diatom, as we have seen, is hard and brit-

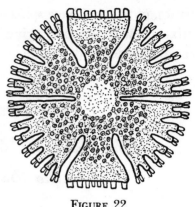

FIGURE 22
Micrasterias

tle. But, as if these differences were not sufficient to enable one to tell them apart, there is a third feature which is characteristic of the Desmids, and that is their duplicate symmetry. In other words, they consist (as shown in Figures 21-22-23) of two similar halves, which are related like an object and its mirror image, spreading from a mid-zone, usually constricted, and called the isthmus, in which lies the nucleus.

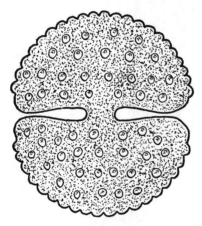

FIGURE 23
Cosmarium

There are some one thousand species of Desmids and as you observe them through the microscope you will be astonished at their great diversity of form and exquisitely sculptured walls, which may be finely striated or roughened by minute dots or points or perhaps by wart-like elevations or even by spines of different shapes. Their edges too, may be even or notched, or prolonged into teeth, or variously cut and divided. These ornaments, together with their graceful form and beautiful green color, make the Desmids objects of great beauty, and a source of never-ending delight to the microscopist.

Although both the Desmids and Diatoms are spread chiefly by movements of the water, they both, nevertheless, have the ability to move about from place to place under their own power, as it were, which they do by the aid of projecting threads worked against the ground. You may see them move as you observe them through the microscope, when you will find that the Desmids move rather stately and slowly in one direction, whereas the Diatoms may travel quickly half-way across the field of view, and then for no apparent reason may abruptly retrace their course or dart off obliquely on a new one. Both of these groups of plants reproduce by division, the Diatoms usually lengthwise and the Desmids at the isthmus, the two halves thus formed each regenerating the missing part.

A striking feature of many Desmids, especially in the crescent-shaped ones, is the presence, in each extremity, of a small colorless, spherical space or vacuole, containing minute granules or crystals which are in constant vibration. This movement is the famous Brownian movement * which can be observed when

* *It was discovered by a botanist, Robert Brown, in 1827, and named after him.*

any finely divided insoluble substance suspended in water is examined under the microscope, and results from the vibration of the molecules of the surrounding liquid. Such molecules are in constant motion and when they strike against one another, they rebound. Some of them strike against the suspended particles and tend to displace them, but inasmuch as the molecular bombardment is from all sides, the suspended particles are not apt to be moved unless they are of very small size. Accordingly, as in the case of the crystals contained in the vacuoles, a larger number of impacts on one side will necessarily cause a light particle to be displaced, only, however, to be pushed in another direction in the next instance.

ADVENTURE 11

We Find Beauty in Unexpected Places

All living things are made up of units of protoplasm, a substance which has been called the "physical basis of life." The units are known as cells and range in number from one, in the simplest plants and animals, to millions in the higher forms of plant and animal life. In the simplest plants and animals, such as the Amœba, Euglena and the Diatoms and Desmids, which we have already examined, the cells perform all the activities essential to the life of the individual, but in the higher plants and animals, the cells are differentiated into different kinds, each kind performing some particular function and all dependent upon one another.

Now there are instances where the cells which form some of the simplest plants, instead of being separate and free, like the Diatoms and Desmids, are grouped together in large numbers and held together by a gelatinous secretion from their walls, forming what is known as a colony. Such colonial formations are the Algæ of which some twelve hundred species are known. They are very widely distributed over the face of the earth, some living in the water, either attached or floating, some on land, and some indifferently in either.

The shining green scum which is to be found on the surface of ponds and streams or attached like soft green clouds to sticks and stones and dead leaves is Algæ and though perhaps repulsive in appearance is not quite as bad as it looks. As a matter of fact, under the microscope it reveals a beauty literally undreamed of. Suppose we take some home and examine it. With a dissecting needle we unravel some of it and find that it comes in little thread-like formations. If we now take one of these threads and examine it through the microscope, being sure to keep it moist—otherwise it will dry and shrivel up—we will find that it looks like a beautiful string of green beads. All of the beads, which are the cells, look alike, for each is capable of a separate existence; but through one of Nature's whims they have become fastened together.

If we focus our attention on one of these individual cells (Figure 24) we will find how it is made up. Most abundant, though not always the most prominent, is the cytoplasm, a term given to all the protoplasm which is outside of the nucleus. This cytoplasm, which seems generally to be of the consistency of a viscous liquid, is clearly the working part of the cell—that which transports materials, builds the walls, produces chemical reactions and the like. Next in prominence is the nucleus, a rounded body of denser but still gelatinous consistency lying in the cytoplasm. This is the

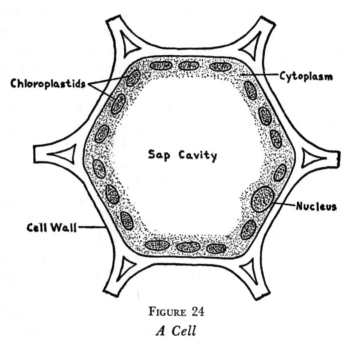

FIGURE 24

A Cell

control organ of the cell, exerting upon the work of the cytoplasm an influence which guards the building of the organism along the general lines of its heredity. If by any chance you are unable to see the nucleus, place a few filaments of the Algæ in a solution of eosin and add a few drops of acetic acid to give the solution a pale rose color. After twenty to thirty minutes examine again, when the nucleus will be stained a deep red. Scattered throughout the cytoplasm are the chloroplasts, also of denser gelatinous consistency with rounded forms and containing the green coloring matter which most plants contain. These chloroplasts are the factories where the food is made for the plant; here the raw food materials are taken in and transformed, by means of the green coloring matter called chlorophyll and the action of sunlight through complex chemical reactions, into certain foods that are thence transported to various parts of the plant. In young and small cells the cytoplasm occupies the entire cell, but as they grow older and larger, rifts, filled with sap composed of various substances in solutions,

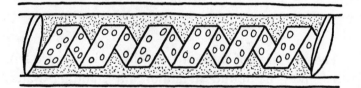

FIGURE 25
Spirogyra

occur in the cytoplasm, and eventually these rifts enlarge and run together until they form a single great central sap-filled cavity. And finally there is the cell wall, composed of a firm elastic water-permeable substance called cellulose, whose obvious function is to enclose this microscopic thing of wonder. If you have any difficulty in distinguishing the cell wall, drop a little glycerine or salt water on the slide. This will cause the cell contents to shrink and bring out the wall.

One of the most interesting of the many species of Algæ is Spirogyra (Figure 25). It usually grows in masses, forming the soft green clouds apparently floating just under the surface of the water. Sometimes it may also be found on the under side of the leaves of underwater plants, from which it hangs in long streamers, like certain vines found in the jungles. On examining it through the microscope we shall find that each cell has its bright green chloroplast in the form of a spiral, from which the species gets its name.

FIGURE 26
Oscillatoria

Another Alga of interest is Oscillatoria (Figure 26), which may be found in almost all standing water, where it frequently forms thick floating mats of a dark purplish or almost blackish color. On viewing a filament under the microscope you will find that the cells have the form of short cylinders, which may be even shorter than they are wide. The most striking feature of this species is that the filaments are capable of a swaying or oscillating movement, to which the plant owes its name, and also of a twisting or rotating motion. The filaments are also capable of movement, and if you should place a mass of them on a wet surface you will find that the threads will spread out into a uniform film.

A third and very common species is Vaucheria (Figure 27) which can be found as a damp green mat on the bottom of shallow water, or on wet ground, and resembling felt both to touch and sight.

This species of Algæ reproduces by two methods. In one method, the end of a filament enlarges and becomes club-shaped (Figure 27A), a wall meanwhile growing across the filament at the base of the club. In this club-shaped part a spore is now formed from the contents and shortly escapes by the rupture of the free end of the filament. This spore, (Figure 27B) which is large enough to be visible to the naked eye, is capable of swimming about, by means of rapidly vibrating little threads, or cilia, and after doing so for a time finally settles down and germinates, sending out one or more tubes which develop into typical Vaucheria filaments.

In the second method, a short branch grows out from the side of a filament into a small ovoid cell, the

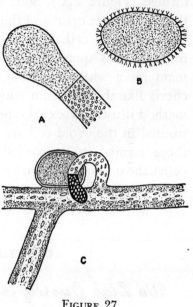

FIGURE 27
Vaucheria

contents of which are cut off from the rest of the fila
ment by a cross wall, as in the first method. Close to
this cell, a smaller narrow, curved or coiled tube is
formed (Figure 27C). Soon the free ends of each of
these structures open and the contents of the tube pass
into the ovoid cell, in which a spore without cilia is
formed. This spore is liberated and after lying dormant for a while eventually germinates into a Vaucheria like the one from which it sprang. This second
method illustrates sexual reproduction for the contents
formed in the ovoid cell are eggs, (female cells) while
those formed in the coiled tube, are sperms (male
cells), the union of the two being known as fertilization.

ADVENTURE 12

We Stab Ourself for Love of Science

Those of you who enjoy reading mystery stories, and
I must confess that I have a liking myself for that type
of writing, perhaps recall some tale of horror wherein
the story hinges on whether a reddish stain found near
the scene of the "crime" is, as the fictional detective
supposes, blood. If, on examination, it is found to be
blood, and therefore a clue of "paramount importance," it enables the detective after some three hundred pages of fumbling about to arrive finally at a
solution. Joking aside, the examination of blood stains
found on the scene of a murder often *is* of major im-

portance in actual police work. I do not suggest that we become amateur detectives and hie ourselves to the scene of the next murder we read of in the papers and offer our services to the regular police, but I think that it may be of interest, and perhaps some fun, to know how blood stains are determined as such and to examine such stains for ourselves.

First, however, we should know what blood consists of, so our first step is to examine some of it. I am afraid that I shall have to ask you to stab yourself but don't be alarmed, as it will be a painless operation and do you no harm—if you follow one necessary precaution. Take a slide and cover glass and clean them thoroughly. Then bathe one thumb in alcohol, sterilize a sharp needle by heating it in a flame, and with it prick the back of the thumb. Place a small drop of the resulting blood on the slide and quickly put on the cover glass. To prevent evaporation you might surround the edges of the cover glass with a little vaseline.

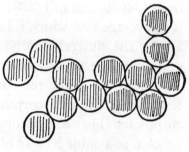

FIGURE 28
Red Blood Corpuscles

Our next step is to transfer the slide to the stage of the microscope and examine it. We shall find a number of circular flattened discs floating about (Figure 28). The center of each disc appears darker than the rim, but this darker shade is merely the effect of refraction resulting from the double concave form of the disc. As we watch these discs we observe that they show a tendency to approach each other, adhering and forming what may appear to be a pile of coins or, if the stratum of blood is not sufficiently thick to permit such an arrangement, they may partially overlap one another or perhaps simply adhere to one another by their edges.

These little discs are known as red blood corpuscles. In man they are circular in shape, as we have just seen, and so are those of most of the higher mammals except the camel tribe which has oval red corpuscles, as have also birds, reptiles and fishes. In size the corpuscles of various animals differ greatly. In the frog, for instance, they measure 1/1108 inch, while in man they measure 1/3200 inch. Even in the same blood they are not altogether uniform in size; thus in man they may vary from 1/4000 inch to 1/2800. Generally, however, there is an average size, which is fairly constantly maintained among the different individuals of the same species, that of man being, as I have said, 1/3200 inch.

In addition to the red corpuscles we may observe a few smaller circular corpuscles. These are the white corpuscles. They are far outnumbered by the red corpuscles, in a cubic inch of blood from a healthy human being numbering but a mere quarter of a million to eighty millions of the red. Unlike the red which vary greatly in size in the different species of the vertebrated animals, the size of the white is extremely constant, measuring about 1/3000 inch in the warm-blooded animals and 1/2500 inch in reptiles.

As we watch these white corpuscles under the microscope we may frequently see them behave in the manner of the Amœba,* undergoing changes of form and even moving from place to place. When thus moving they engulf particles which lie in their course and afterwards eject them in the same manner.

And now that we have examined fresh blood and found out what it consists of, let us see how a stain suspected to be one of blood is so determined. Unless you have some sort of material already stained with blood, you will have to manufacture such a stain before you can proceed. In that event, take a piece of cloth and stain it with a drop of blood from your thumb, taking the same precautions as you did above, and let it dry thoroughly. When thoroughly dried, scrape off a little of the stain on a slide. You may have to cut a little of the cloth but this will not interfere with the test and if you should happen to find a stain on some wood you may find it necessary to scrape off some of the wood fibers along with the dried blood. To the dried stain on the slide, next add a few drops of a very weak salt solution and heat over a flame until the solution has been entirely evaporated and a reddish-brown residue remains. Then apply a cover glass and flood the preparation

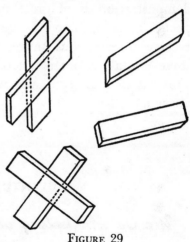

Figure 29
Hemin Crystals

* See Adventure 7.

45

with as much acetic acid as will remain in place under the cover. Heat again until the acetic acid boils. After the acid has evaporated, and when the slide is dry and cool, place on the stage of the microscope and examine. You should find a number of crystals—minute, narrow rhombic plates of dark-brown color (Figure 29). They vary in size and may lie simply across one another, or in stellate groups.

These crystals (known as hemin crystals) are positive evidence that the stain is of blood and hence their demonstration is of great importance in stains suspected of being blood. I must add, however, lest you receive an erroneous impression, that the presence of these crystals is not a test of *human* blood; all they prove is that the stain was made by the blood of an animal.

ADVENTURE 13

We Go Marketing with a Honey Bee

The Honey Bee is a common and abundant insect in summer and you have no doubt often seen it buzzing about some flower. But aside from giving it a wide berth for fear of being stung, did you ever consider what it might be doing about such a flower? Now the answer is a very simple one, for in addition to seeking the nectar which plants provide as food for many insects, the bee is also obtaining food for the young back in the hive; in other words, doing her marketing. And, as if she had anticipated the bee's need for some means of transporting such food, Nature has provided the bee with baskets in which to carry home her purchases. I use the word "purchases" in the literal sense, for the bee does not merely pilfer what she wants from the defenceless flower; she really pays for what she takes by carrying pollen from one flower to another, thus effecting what is known as cross-pollination, which is so essential to the continued vigor and fertility of all flowering plants.

We are not interested just now in cross-pollination, but in the baskets which the bee carries. Her baskets are not such as we use but are differently designed, yet admirably suited to serve the same purpose as those made for our use.

To examine these baskets and find out what they look like, it is necessary for us to capture a bee and subject it to the deadly fumes of our lethal chamber, so that we may do so without fear of being stung. We follow the same procedure as we employed in capturing Musca; * and when all signs of life have passed we take it out of the lethal chamber and glance at the hind legs. Attached to them we should find on each one a roundish mass of a yellowish sticky substance. This is the pollen dust which the bee had gathered—the flour which she had "purchased" and which was to have made the "bread" for the baby bees back in the hive. At this point do not consider me a cold-blooded villain for suggesting that we take the life of the "mother" bee and thus leave the baby bees with the dismal pros-

* See Adventure 6.

pect of starving to death, as that, I can assure you, is
not so. On her failure to return home they will immediately be taken in hand by some other bee and
brought up in the proper manner.

Removing the pollen from one of the legs by means

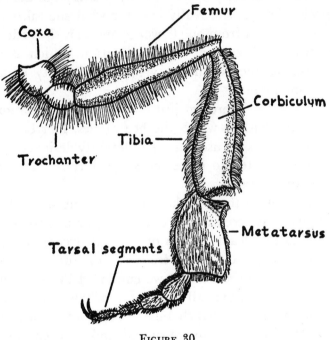

FIGURE 30
Leg of a Honey Bee

of a small brush, we sever the leg from the body, place
it on a slide, and view it through the microscope. We
shall find that it consists of three large regions called
the femur, tibia and some smaller ones called the tarsal
segments, the first of these being called the metatarsus.
Now if we examine the tibia we will find that it is fash-

ioned into a sort of receptacle (Figure 30). This is the basket, or corbiculum as it is scientifically called, in which the bee carries her "purchases."

How does she fill these baskets? That is a question you may well ask. As the bee climbs over the flower, the flexible branching hairs, with which the body and legs are covered, entangle the pollen grains. By means of special structures, called pollen combs (Figure 31) and located on the inner surface of the hind tarsus, the bee combs the pollen grains out of the hairs and transfers them to the baskets, at the same time pressing the pollen down into the baskets by means of the auricle (Figure 31), so as to fill them to the maximum amount they can contain.

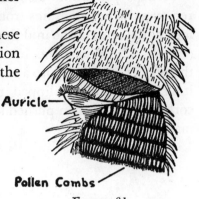

Auricle

Pollen Combs

FIGURE 31
Pollen Combs

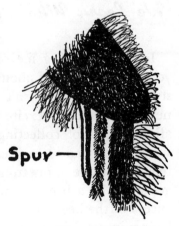

Spur

FIGURE 32
Spur

If you have a reading lens (and they can be bought very inexpensively) you might watch a bee as it climbs about a flower, and then you will see for yourself just how she collects and places the pollen in her baskets.

Perhaps you would also like to know how the bee removes the pollen grains from her baskets. If you will look at the apex of the middle tibia you will find a spur (Figure 32). When the bee arrives at the hive she thrusts her hind legs into a cell and with the spur pries it off, the spur being slipped in at the upper end of the corbiculum and then pushed along the tibia under the mass of pollen.*

ADVENTURE 14

We Learn What It Means to be Stung

In accompanying me on our last adventure, were you somewhat timid about doing so for fear of being stung? There really isn't any danger if you are not nervous and do not excite your intended victim, for in all my years of collecting insects I have only been stung twice, and in each case by a wasp that managed to get up inside of my trouser leg. But should you ever get stung by a bee, you will find it a painful experience. For the bee, too, it would be a most unfortunate happening and in all probability it would never live to tell the tale.

When Nature set out to create all the different animals that inhabit the globe, she realized the need of

See Adventure 51 for other structures.

providing each and every one with some means of defense against its enemies. But when she created the Honey Bee she must have had one of those mental lapses that we sometimes have, when we do some foolish thing, for she provided it with a weapon that when used acted as a boomerang and usually with fatal results.

To anticipate your questions, how? and why?, let us examine the stinging apparatus of a Honey Bee. Then we shall find the answer. If you have retained the specimen you used for our last adventure and it has not become dried and brittle it will serve very well; otherwise you will have to secure a fresh one.

To remove the stinging apparatus requires some technique, if we are to do more than merely snip it off close to the body with our scissors. If we take the dead insect and hold it between our thumb and forefinger, gently pressing on the abdomen, we shall find that the stinging apparatus can be pulled out with our tweezers. It is rather a delicate operation, but if performed carefully you will be able to remove the poison glands and duct along with the stinger itself.

Placing the entire stinging apparatus on a slide, we examine it through the microscope. We find that it is something of a miniature hypodermic needle, albeit a rather complicated structure. The entire apparatus consists, as shown in Figure 33, of a sheath, a pair of sting feelers or palpi, a reservoir, and a pair of glands, one acid and the other alkaline.

The action of the sting is rather complex but briefly it is somewhat as follows: first, a suitable place is selected on the body of the victim with the help of the

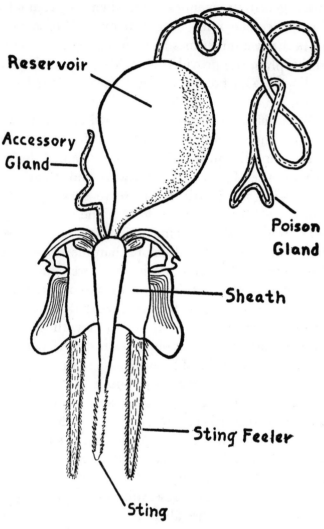

Reservoir

Accessory
Gland

Poison
Gland

Sheath

Sting Feeler

Sting

FIGURE 33
Sting of Honey Bee

palpi or feelers and when such a place is found the sheath opens up a wound. As soon as a wound has been opened, the two barbed darts are thrust forward, striking in alternately and interrupted at intervals by the deeper plunging of the sheath. Meanwhile, a poisonous secretion from the poison gland has become mixed, in the reservoir, with a secretion from the accessory gland, and as the sheath is plunged deeper into the wound this mixture is conducted by a duct into the channel of the sheath through which it passes into the wound. It is said that both fluids are necessary for a deadly effect, and that in insects which simply paralyze their prey as the solitary wasps, the alkaline glands are functionless.

If you will now look closely at the darts you will see that each has a number of barbed teeth, which are so formed as to prevent the withdrawal of the sting from the wound. Accordingly when a bee stings, it finds that it can extricate itself from its victim only by leaving its sting behind. Now if the bee could only cast off that part of the sting that was in the wound, as a starfish casts off one of its arms when caught in some inextricable manner, all would be well. But the bee unfortunately cannot do this, but must leave the entire stinging apparatus in the wound, thus suffering internal injuries which usually prove fatal.

It is only the worker bees, however, that are thus affected. The sting of the queen bees, and also of wasps, is devoid of barbed teeth, and the sting can be pulled out of a wound without difficulty. These insects, therefore, can sting with impunity, as far as they themselves are concerned.

We Meet with an Optical Illusion

While examining the Algæ, in our eleventh adventure, did you observe perched on one of the threads, or swimming through the microscopic jungle, strange little animals carrying about with them what appeared to be wheels that seemed to be constantly in motion (Figure 34)? If you did, then you found what are called Rotifers or "wheel-bearers," animals which belong to a remarkable family of microscopic creatures called collectively the Rotifera, from the Latin *rota,* a wheel, and *fero,* I carry.

Actually, of course, the Rotifers do not carry wheels about with them and what appear to be such are in reality two discs or lobes bearing marginal wreaths of fine thin thread-like motile organs or cilia, which vibrate so rapidly that the effect is one of a rotating wheel. The motion of the cilia suggests the whirling of electric ventilators, such as are found in the windows of some kitchens to suck out the overheated air, for the purpose of the cilia is to create in the water a current which sucks the minute organisms that serve as food into the animal's mouth. They are also used for locomotion, propelling the creature through the water much in the fashion of a motor-boat propeller.

The Rotifers are very common and abundant and may be found in almost any pond or shallow body of still water, hiding among the leaflets or in masses of various water plants such as Ceratophyllum. They may be easily and quickly obtained by taking a portion of one of these plants from the collecting bottle, in which you carried home your material for examination, and rinsing it in a watchglass full of some of the pond water, when the Rotifers will be washed from among the leaflets. A drop of this water transferred to a slide with the dipping tube should then reveal several of these microscopic animals.

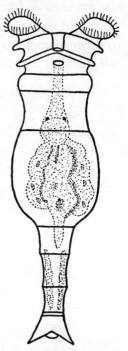

Most of the Rotifers are cylindrical in form but there are some that are oblong in shape and still others resemble flat discs. In some forms the body may be soft and flexible; in others it may be enclosed within a shell-like coating or cuticle. At one end is the head; at the other a long tail-like

FIGURE 34

Philodina

part called the foot, which is used as a rudder to guide the Rotifer when swimming, or as an anchor against the propelling power of the cilia when it desires to hunt for food. It can adhere to objects by means of a secretion from a cement gland. In some Rotifers the foot is composed of rings which slide into one another like the sections of a spy-glass, thus permitting the animal to fold itself up into a smaller compass. This is perhaps of some advantage for, in addition to swimming, such Rotifers can also crawl or creep about in

55

the manner of a measuring worm by alternate contractions and extensions of the foot. If you should happen to capture such a species you can observe this for yourself, for you will find that the Rotifer can travel with a surprising rapidity and cover considerable microscopic distances in a relatively short time.

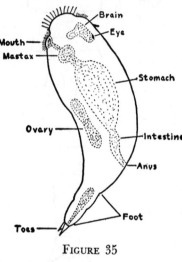

FIGURE 35

Anatomy of a Rotifer

The mouth is usually located between the two ciliary discs near the center of the front part of the body, although in some forms it is on the lower surface of the animal. From the mouth a tubular passage leads into a region called the mastax or chewing stomach, where are located a pair of jaws which are constantly at work, breaking up the food. With a low power objective the action of these jaws can be seen through the transparent tissues of the animal, and is a sure way of distinguishing a living Rotifer from other organisms. From the mastax the food passes into a glandular stomach, where it is digested, the undigested particles passing through the intestine and out through the anus (Figure 35).

The sexes of the Rotifers are separate, and reproduction is by eggs, which are usually semi-transparent, smooth, ovoid bodies. They may be dropped anywhere or they may be attached to a leaf or some other aquatic object. Sometimes they remain fastened to the outside posterior part of the parent and are thus carried about until the young are detached.

There are quite a number of different species of Rotifers. A common species is Philodina, which is so abundant that almost any drop of water from the proper localities is sure to contain one or more of them. Its white, rather thick, spindle-shaped body, its constantly moving jaws, and its creeping movement, after the fashion of a measuring worm, are characteristics that make it easily identifiable and you should have no trouble in spotting it almost instantly.

Most of the Rotifers are free-swimming but there are some that do not swim at all. These live their entire lives in tubular houses which they build and attach to water plants. One of these, which goes by the some-what girlish name of Melicerta (Figure 36), is a brick-maker, mason and architect combined, building herself a chimney-like house out of little mud balls, which she fashions one by one and adds to the circular wall. Melicerta's home is just large enough to be seen

FIGURE 36
Melicerta

57

with the naked eye, and you may find it if you look carefully on the under-side of the leaves of various water plants.

The manner in which Melicerta builds her house is most interesting to watch. If you will observe carefully you will find that the ciliary disc, which consists of four parts or lobes of different shapes and sizes, creates three distinct currents in the water. One current is directed towards the mouth where the acceptable morsels of food are selected and passed on to the mastax; a second is directed away from the mouth for the purpose of carrying away rejected fragments; and a third is directed in toward a small cavity where the little mud balls or pellets which she uses in building her house are fashioned. Into this cavity the building material is poured and turned about rapidly by fine cilia which line it. An adhesive secretion is also added and this causes the particles to adhere to one another while the revolving motion makes the balls spherical. When a ball has been fashioned and is ready to be deposited in the place intended for it, Melicerta rotates or twists herself in her tubular house, bends her body forward, and deposits the ball or pellet on the top row of the circular wall and there cements it fast with an invisible insoluble cement. This building process seems to be almost a continuous one for as she grows her house must needs be enlarged to accommodate the increase in her size. Of course, a point is eventually reached when she will grow no more, and then all building activities cease.

The Rotifers are truly among the most fascinating

of all the living things you will find in the microscopic world, and once you have made the acquaintance of some of the more common species you will be eager to hunt for the rarer forms.

An odd peculiarity of the Rotifers is their power to resist desiccation. If dried slowly certain species secrete gelatinous envelopes which prevent further drying, and in such a condition they may not only live through seasons of drought but also may be subjected to extremes of temperature without perishing.

ADVENTURE 16

We Make the Acquaintance of Eylais

While in the process of collecting material from your favorite pond or pool you have undoubtedly seen what you thought were spiders moving rapidly through the water or forcing themselves among the leaflets of water plants. They are not spiders, however, although they do look something like them, but water-mites. Sometimes they are erroneously called water-spiders, although this name is not a good one, as there are some true spiders that are semi-aquatic in habit and therefore more deserving of such a name.

The water-mites are quite active little animals, swimming freely and actively through the water by means of eight legs attached to the forward part of the body. They are all usually visible to the naked eye, and may be obtained either by capturing them with a bottle as they swim about or by submerging the bottle and letting some of the water plants float into it. Such mites as may have been hiding among the plants will then be carried into the bottle from which they may be removed as desired by a dipping tube. A very common water-mite of our ponds is a red species known by the name of Eylais. (Figure 37). It is rather large in size and for the most part may be studied with a comparatively low-power objective.

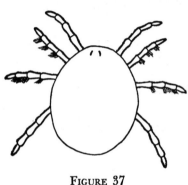

FIGURE 37

Eylais

The water-mites are rather plump little animals, oval or nearly spherical in outline, with a skin which is usually soft and easily broken, and brightly, if not brilliantly colored in various shades of crimson, yellow, blue, brown, green or purple. The upper part may be entirely smooth, or densely clothed with short hairs, or perhaps covered only with a few scattered fine bristles.

They feed on small crustacea and minute insect larvæ, the mouth being usually a complicated affair and always having short jointed palpi or feelers. The eyes, which may be two or four in number, are generally on the upper surface near the front border, and rather small in size. The legs, which are eight in number, are long and jointed, the last joint ending in one or two short claws, and are covered with many long hairs which help in swimming. On the under surface, you may notice one or more very small dark spots. These are the external openings of the air-tubes or tracheae which ramify through the body and supply it with oxygen which is obtained from the air, for although the water-mites can remain under water for long periods, they must come to the surface every now and then to breathe.

The water-mites reproduce by eggs which may frequently be seen as small brownish jelly-masses attached to the stems of water plants or to the lower surface of floating leaves. In most species the newly hatched young, which often bear no resemblance at all to their parents, are free living like the adults, but in some instances they are parasitic on aquatic insects and become independent only when they are full grown.

ADVENTURE 17

We Take a Lesson in Food Analysis

In the manufacture or preparation of foodstuffs, impurities such as dust or bacteria often enter into the products either through accident or carelessness. Frequently foreign substances are added through design. In such instances the substances are known as adulterants.

An adulterant very commonly used is starch. Now there are various kinds of starches, such as potato, corn, wheat, rice and tapioca, to name but a few, and the first thing the food analyst must learn is to be able to recognize the various grains under the microscope. Forunately they are easily obtained and as easily observed and we should not have any difficulty in learning to distinguish the different grains for they are usually constant in their characteristics.

We shall begin by examining potato starch, for its grains are large and possess certain definite features which may or may not be present in the grains of the other starches. With a knife we gently scrape the newly cut surface of a potato and transfer some of the potato substance (a mere speck will suffice) to a slide, to which we add a drop of water and then cover with a cover glass. Placing the slide on the stage of the microscope, we examine the potato substance and find countless oval—or ellipsoidal, or even triangular-shaped—almost transparent bodies which look like miniature oyster shells (Figure 38A). These are the potato starch grains. As the grains are not flat we must slowly rotate the fine adjustment to and fro so as to obtain all the parts in focus. Near one extremity (usually the narrower) we shall find a minute dark spot, which is not in the center of the grain, called the hilum. This is the oldest part of the starch grain, around which the remainder of the shell has grown layer by layer, until fully formed. If we focus up and down around this point, we shall find concentric lines or rings, called striations, which indicate the layers where the grain has grown larger and larger.

Unlike those of the potato starch, the grains of wheat starch, which we examine next, have neither a hilum or striations (Figure 38B). These grains are large in size and oval or rounded in outline and under

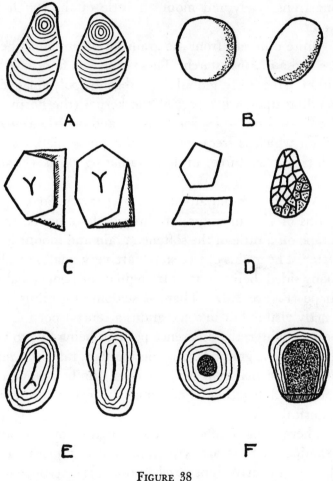

FIGURE 38
Starch Grains

the microscope look somewhat like flattened pebbles. Wheat starch appears on the market either as lumps, angular granules, or a fine powder. If unable to obtain the commercial starch, procure some wheat grains and soak them in water for twenty-four hours. Then cut one transversely and mount a little of the starch in water.

Quite different from the grains of potato and wheat are those of corn starch. These you will find may be either irregularly globular or sharply polygonal, depending upon what part of the kernel (the horny or floury portion) they come from, and with a central hilum which is frequently a point but sometimes exhibiting two, three, or four radiating clefts (Figure 38C).

We next turn our attention to rice starch. Soak a few grains of rice in water for three or four hours, then scrape off a little of the softened grain and mount it in water. The grains of rice starch are very small and also many sided, being square, triangular, or pentagonal in shape (Figure 38D). There is seldom any hilum distinctly visible but in some grains a central portion appears brighter, the difference perhaps being due to the drying of the grain. Among the angular grains you may find larger masses consisting of a number of grains compacted together. These may be ovoid or nearly spherical in shape.

There are a number of other starches you may also examine such as arrowroot, bean and tapioca. The shape of the arrowroot starch grains varies according to the plant from which it was derived, for this starch does not all come from one kind of plant. The starch grains of the common bean are for the most part ellipsoidal or kidney-shaped, with a conspicuous irregular branching cleft running out from the center and appearing black because of enclosed air (Figure 38E), while those of tapioca are usually kettle-drum or sugar-loaf shaped according to whether they rest on their flat surfaces or on their sides (Figure 38F). The hilum is central and is usually a point or small cleft, and often a triangular enlargement of the hilum extends to the flattened surface.

ADVENTURE 18

We Raid Our Kitchen

Now that we have become familiar with the appearance of starch of various kinds, which is, as I have said, a common adulterant in foods, we can proceed to a little detective work.

We shall begin with butter, which is perhaps not the most interesting object for the microscope but which is easy to examine and so will give us a start. Place a small sample upon a clean slide, add a drop of olive oil, and cover the whole with a cover glass which should be pressed down firmly until the specimen forms a thin film or layer. First of all, we look for starch grains which should be absent. Having finally satisfied ourselves as to their presence or absence, we next turn our attention to the drops of water, which we observe, and which by their amount and size indicate the quality of butter. Should we find but a few scattered drops of various sizes we know that the butter is of high quality. Should we find, however, that the water globules are all very small and all apparently of the same size, we know that the butter is milk-blended, while should we find unusually large drops, we then have evidence that the butter contains an excessive amount of water.

We next turn our attention to flour, which is sometimes adulterated with other starches, such as potato starch, the grains of which are quite characteristic, as we have seen, and which we should have no difficulty in finding if they are present. Flour also frequently contains impurities, such as the remains of various grain insects and you might do well to look for such substances.

Cocoa is another food that is often adulterated with foreign starches, such as wheat and arrowroot, and if they are present you should be able to detect them quite easily.

Jams, marmalades and other preserves are foods that are also frequently adulterated. There is a case on record where grass seeds were found in artificial raspberry jam in place of the natural fruit seeds. A common adulterant in jam is apple pulp which can often be identified by searching for pieces of the tough membrane from the core. This has a very characteristic appearance under the microscope (Figure 39).

Honey is another food which you may profitably examine for the purpose of knowing how to distinguish genuine honey from the artificial variety, manu-factured from various sugars. This kind of honey contains no pollen grains,* so if you find these absent in the specimen you examine, you have every right to view the honey with suspicion. When dissolved in water, genuine honey gives a residue consisting almost entirely of pollen grains so that extraneous matter, as pieces of wood and fibers, are easily recognized. An-other test is to look for starch grains which often occur in artificial honey but never in that made by bees.

Sometimes substances are added to cream in order

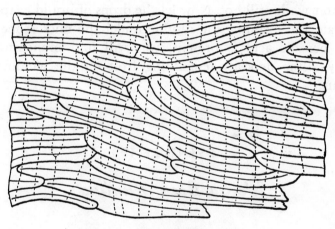

FIGURE 39
Membrane (Endocarp) of Apple

to thicken it, the thickness of the cream being the pop-ular criterion of its richness in fat. A common adulter-ant is *agar-agar,* a substance resembling gelatin in its properties and obtained from a Japanese seaweed. To

* *For the nature of pollen grains, see Adventure 47.*

detect the presence of *agar-agar,* boil a little cream with five per cent sulphuric acid, add a few crystals of potassium permanganate and allow to settle. Then examine some of the sediment for diatoms * and if you find any of these microscopic plants *agar-agar* is probably present.

Preservatives are sometimes added to various foods, the most common being, perhaps, benzoic acid. To detect the presence of this preservative, place a portion of the material to be tested on a watch glass and cover with a glass plate. Heat to boiling over a flame, allowing the steam to condense on the plate, and remove the latter while still hot. Now let the drops of liquid evaporate and examine the residue under the microscope. If benzoic acid is present, you will find branching crystalline deposits resembling frost on the window pane.

ADVENTURE 19

We Go Bear Hunting

For our nineteenth adventure we are going bear hunting—not the four-legged rambling creature that inhabits our northern forests, but a small microscopic animal that is to be found on the bottom of shallow ponds, known as a Water Bear.

As the Water Bears are quite invisible to the naked eye, measuring less than one-sixteenth of an inch, the

* *For the nature of diatoms see Adventure 9.*

only way we can obtain one is to take home some of the bottom mud from a shallow pool and examine it under the microscope a little at a time, being sure to spread it out on the slide so as to permit light to shine through it. It may take some time to find one, as they are not any too numerous, but to obtain one of them will, I think, amply repay your efforts.

The Water Bears are queer little animals and zoologists are not quite sure how to classify them. They are usually, however, placed with the spiders and mites because of their four pairs of short hooked legs, which is the only characteristic that entitles them to be classified with such animals.

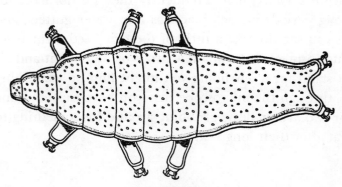

FIGURE 40
Water Bear

The Water Bear looks very much like a new-born puppy (Figure 40), with a body that is soft, colorless and transparent. It is very slow of movement, for this reason often being called a Tardigrade. Besides living at the bottom of shallow ponds it may also be found on tree trunks, in moss, and even in the debris in ditches.

It feeds on bits of decayed vegetation, the mouth being a small opening at the front of the part representing the head, on each side of which there is usually a small eye. A short distance behind the mouth the so-called gizzard can easily be seen through the transparent body.

The Water Bears are among the "toughest" animals that we may ever expect to find, for they can be dried and shriveled up into nothing more than a grain of powder, and after existing in such a condition for months may be brought back to life merely by being placed in some water. They may even be heated to 250 degrees Fahrenheit. Frequently they lie dormant for long periods in such places as rain water gutters, and if you should take a little of the dried sediment from such a place and add a few drops of water to it and let it stand for a few hours you might find on examining it through the microscope that you have captured one or two Water Bears grubbing around for something to eat after their long fast.

ADVENTURE 20

We Discover a Zoological Radio Station

Life would not be what it is if we were not vexed by petty annoyances of one kind or another. For the most part they are of a trifling nature, but oftentimes they become a real nuisance. Take the mosquito, for instance, as a case in point.

Personally I am not overly bothered by this biting insect, although I must admit that sometimes it can become quite pestiferous; but I know many people to whom it is a source of much discomfort, causing not only physical suffering but also mental distress. My wife is one of these unfortunates and the presence of just one individual in the bedroom is sufficient to cause her a sleepless night. I have often been amused to see her, just before retiring, take her Flit gun in hand and set out on a "big game" expedition. But to her it is no laughing matter.

Aside from being an annoyance, the mosquito is also a real menace to health, for it has been convicted of carrying yellow fever and malaria. I would not worry about catching either of these diseases, for yellow fever has been brought under control and moreover is limited to the warmer regions of the south where it is now a rarity. Almost the same can be said for malaria, for rapid strides have been made in recent years towards the eradication of this disease by various preventive measures. One thing to be thankful for is that only one United States species has been convicted of transmitting malaria. This species goes by the impressive name of *Anopheles quadrimaculatus* and perhaps you might like to know how to recognize it should you ever meet it. Well, it is easy enough, for the female has a beak that appears to be three-pronged and her wings are spotted. There is no harm in being bitten by an Anopheles, unless the insect has had recent access to a malarious person, for the presence of this mosquito does not necessarily mean that there is malaria about. Still it is always wise to be careful and to avoid Anopheles whenever you can.

In spite of his misdeeds, the mosquito is an interesting insect to study, especially under the microscope.

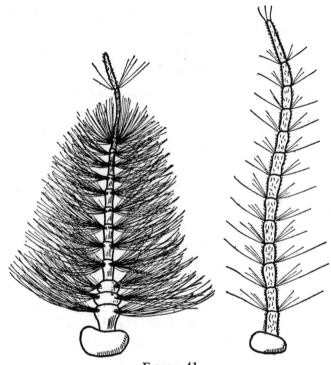

FIGURE 41

Mosquito Antennæ

Try to obtain a male and a female and compare them, to note certain differences. One difference is that the mouth parts of the female are designed for sucking, whereas those of the male are rudimentary, so that it is only the female of the species that can bite. Another difference is in the antennæ. If you refer to Figure 41 when examining your specimens, you will quickly perceive the difference. The antennæ of the male are highly developed organs of hearing and are made up of delicate fibrillæ of various lengths, some of which are thrown into sympathetic vibrations by the note of the female. They act perhaps after the fashion of a radio aerial in picking up sound waves, and are used to locate the female.*

The young or larvæ of mosquitoes are even more interesting to study than the adults. They are the "wrigglers" (Figure 42) that you have probably seen in rain barrels. They may be found in almost any pond or pool and may also be collected by putting a pail of water out in the yard. A week or so later the water should be full of them.

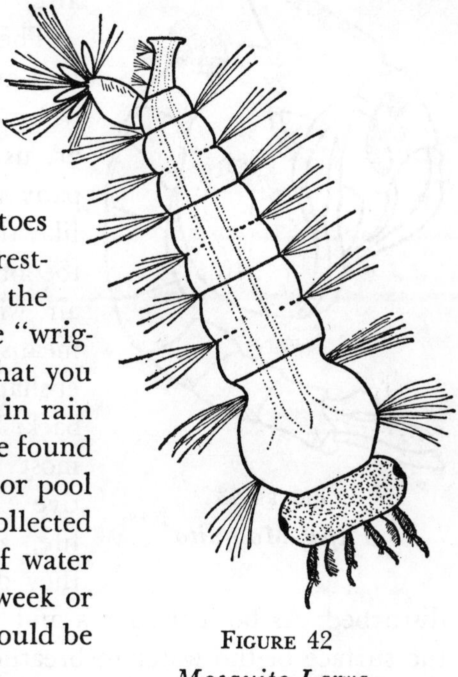

FIGURE 42
Mosquito Larva

As these wrigglers are quite active, it is necessary that we restrict their activi-

* *See Adventure 51 on use of antennæ in Cecropia Moth; also on the structure of mosquito's mouth parts.*

73

ties as much as possible and so we must use a life slide. As we watch them, we note that every now and then they rise to the top of the water and stick what is a breathing siphon up above the surface, meanwhile hanging head downward. They do this because they are not fitted for a continuous existence in water and every now and then they must come to the surface to breathe atmospheric air.

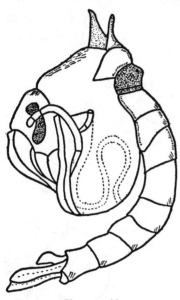

FIGURE 43
Pupa—Mosquito

The pupæ of mosquitoes are the humpbacked wrigglers (Figure 43) that are usually found in company with the larvæ, and like them they also have to breathe atmospheric air, which they take in by means of a pair of trumpet-shaped siphons on the back. Unlike the pupæ of most insects they are active throughout pupal life, although as a rule they do not move unless disturbed. As both the larva and pupa must come to the surface of the water to breathe, we can kill them by putting oil on the surface. They are unable to penetrate the oil film because of surface tension and they soon smother. Try it and see how effectively it works.

74

You might also try and obtain the eggs of mosquitoes. They are laid in a floating raft-like mass and are interesting objects to examine.

ADVENTURE 21

We Come Upon a Strange Partnership

To a person not particularly interested in Nature, the spreading incrustations to be found on rocks, walls, logs, stumps and trees mean nothing. But to those of us who follow rambling trails through field and forest and are on speaking terms with Nature, such incrustations represent one of the most extraordinary groups of plants to be found in the entire plant kingdom.

Such incrustations are called Lichens. Now the Lichens are not individual plants but rather an alliance between two forms of plant life—an Alga and a Fungus—living together in a sort of partnership. The Alga, as we have already seen, is a simple plant, capable of living a free existence and manufacturing its own food. The Fungus, on the other hand, is a parasite; that is, it lives on other plants, stealing its food by means of a network of fine white threads instead of manufacturing it for itself. It must do this in order to survive, for it has lost, you see, the leaf-green granules with which plant-food is manufactured from air, water and mineral salts. But, as we go through life, we find

75

that every loss is offset by some gain. And such is the case with the Fungus; if it has lost the power of making its own food, it has acquired, in recompense, the power of absorbing great quantities of water and of resisting alternate drying and wetting.

As I have said, the Lichen is composed of two different plants—an Alga and a Fungus. In this instance, however, the Fungus is not a parasite, for it does not actually live on the Alga. On the contrary, the two live together in a sort of partnership, each conferring some kind of benefit on the other. Thus, the Alga, by its ability to manufacture food, feeds the Fungus, while the Fungus, by its power to absorb water, is able to supply the Alga with this essential, without which it would perish. Thus they are dependent on one another and without each other they would both die.

Figure 44

Tree Lichen

Lichens may be found all over the world and in a great variety of situations; in fact, they are able to live where few other plants could maintain themselves. A

76

common form is the common Tree Lichen (Figure 44) which grows as a grayish radiate incrustation on the bark of old trees. This Lichen is typical of the closely clinging forms of which many are found also upon rocks as flat spreading patches.

Another very common Lichen is Parmelia, which is more leaf-like in form. This species grows flat on rocks, its pretty gray or green mats dotted with shining brown fruits growing from the center outward in an ever widening circle. A third form, the beautiful scarlet-crested Cladonia, is almost like a miniature shrub, so freely does it branch.

The margins of the Lichens, as you will observe, are much dented and curled, giving them a somewhat leaf-like appearance. This broad, expanded body is the vegetative part and is called the thallus. If you cut a thin section through it and examine it under the microscope you will see just how a Lichen is made up. Should your specimen be too dry and brittle to handle, moisten it by soaking it a short time in water. This will render it more flexible and bring out the green color more clearly.

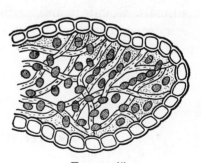

FIGURE 45

Portion of Thallus of a Lichen, Showing Imprisoned Algæ

Viewing it through the microscope, you will find what appears to be a tangle of fine white threads, in which are scattered bits of green. These white threads creep around in search

77

of moisture and also serve to anchor the Lichen to its substratum. The little green bodies are the Algæ and follow wherever the threads might go (See Figure 45).

I am quite sure that you will delight in viewing these strange plants through the microscope, especially the brightly colored species such as Cladonia. The sight that will greet your eyes almost beggars description, and for the moment it will seem as if you had suddenly been transported to fairyland. The cup-shaped or saucer-shaped receptacles, which look like goblets set for a fairy banquet, are the spore cases. The spores are the reproductive part of the Fungus, and though they will germinate without the Alga they will not live without it.

Some Lichens are of economic importance. Various pigments including litmus, are manufactured from some of them, while others serve as food for man and animals. Reindeer and caribou feed on the so-called reindeer-moss, which is not a moss at all but a Lichen, and in Sweden the people at one time made bread of it.

ADVENTURE 22

We Meet Some Relatives of the Amoeba

Like ourselves, a great many animals live in houses, which they either build or find ready-made. We have already seen one instance of this in the case of the Rotifer Melicerta. Another example is Difflugia, which is to be found in the ooze of ponds. It is a relative of the Amœba and like it is a small mass of colorless, or sometimes greenish, protoplasm. Unlike the Amœba, however, it lives within a brown, pear-shaped ovoid or nearly spherical shell, which it builds of minute sand grains and other foreign objects cemented together with the most perfect regularity, every grain fitting exactly in the proper place (Figure 46).

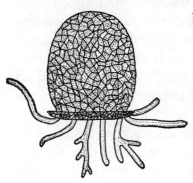

FIGURE 46
Difflugia

There are several species of Difflugia, each with its own characteristic shell. Thus we may find the shell rounded at the top and roughened only by the projecting edges of the sand-grains, or we may find it rounded and bearing several pointed spines, also formed of sand. We may, moreover, find the lower region prolonged as a short neck, at the end of which is the mouth; or we may find it simply rounded as at the top.

FIGURE 47
Arcella

The mouth of the dwelling is circular and may be either smooth or with several rounded teeth. No part of the animal passes through the mouth except the pseudopodia, which are blunt and colorless. Locomotion is effected,

79

as in the Amœba, by the extension and contraction of the pseudopodia, which drag the shell about with the mouth directly downward, and food is captured by them also in the manner of the Amœba.

There is another relative of the Amœba which also lives within a house. This is Arcella which is common in the ooze on vegetation in fresh-water ponds and ditches. Unlike Difflugia, Arcella does not build its home of organic materials but secretes from its own body a brownish shell of delicate membrane which, under the high power of the microscope, is seen to be formed in minute hexagons. When seen from above it appears as a disc with a pale circular spot in the center (Figure 47) from which the pseudopodia protrude, but when seen from a side view it appears more or less dome-shaped.

Both of these animals are worth obtaining and viewing under the microscope, for they are among the most remarkable of our microscopic creatures.

ADVENTURE 23

We Encounter Some Strange Animals

Among the most abundant of all the inhabitants of the microscopic world are the Infusoria, so named because they were first discovered in infusions, that is, water in which animal or vegetable substances had been soaking and decaying. They are one-celled creatures and may be distinguished from other animals by their cilia which serve as locomotor organs and for procuring food.

Infusoria may be found in every body of stagnant or fresh water. Indeed, you need only take a drop of such

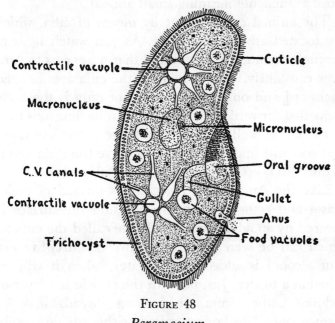

FIGURE 48

Paramecium

water and you will be pretty sure to have captured some form or other. Now there are a great number of species, and unless you make a specialty of studying them, it will be well-nigh impossible to become acquainted with more than a few of the more interesting ones.

A typical and common species is Paramecium (Figure 48). It occurs in fresh water ponds, and, though it

81

may be seen with the naked eye if a proper background is provided, we must usually hunt for it with the microscope. There is no mistaking Paramecium, for it looks very much like a slipper, sometimes being called, because of its shape, the "slipper animalcule," the word animalcule meaning small animal.

The animal swims about by means of cilia, which are located all over the body. As you watch it swim through the water you will find that it appears to turn over constantly. This is because the cilia are inclined backward and obliquely so that not only is the body propelled forward but also rotated in its long axis over to the left as well. Its movements are extremely rapid and you will find it necessary to move the slide about in order to keep it within the field of observation.

Like the Amœba, Paramecium is formed of endoplasm and ectoplasm, and in addition the surface is covered by an additional membrane called the cuticle, which can be seen if a drop or two of thirty-five per cent alcohol is added to the water, when it will be raised as a blister. Just beneath the cuticle is a layer of rod-like bodies from which long threads may be thrown out. The bodies, called trichocysts, are probably weapons of offense and defense. They may be exploded if a little acetic acid is added to the water.

Extending from the forward end, and obliquely backward, is a depression or hollow place resembling the opening in the slipper for the foot. This is called the oral groove and leads to the mouth, located near the center of the lower surface. Paramecium feeds principally on minute organisms which are carried to the mouth by a current of water, created by the cilia in the groove. Passing through the mouth, the food particles are forced down the gullet at the end of which a food vacuole is formed. When fully formed, the food vacuole separates from the gullet and is swept away by a rotary streaming movement of the endoplasm. Digestion occurs within the food vacuole and all undigested material is ejected at a definite anal spot, which is not a permanent opening and can be seen only when the fæces are ejected.

Paramecium reproduces by dividing down the middle, and so rapidly do the young Paramecia grow and so quickly do they divide again that it has been estimated that one Paramecium may be

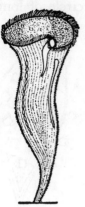

FIGURE 49
Stentor

responsible for 268,000,-000 offspring within a month.

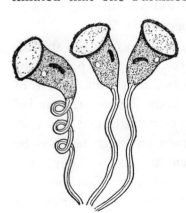

FIGURE 50
Vorticella

Another extremely interesting Infusorium is Stentor (Figure 49) which is often abundant in water about sphagnum moss. This animal, transparent, bluish-green or whitish in color, may be either free-swimming (when it is pear-shaped in form) or attached (when it is trumpet-shaped). In the latter case it is fastened to some object by the narrow end of the body. The entire sur-

83

face of the body is covered with cilia, but they are small and fine. Around the edge of the anterior border is a circle of longer and larger vibratile hairs, which you can see with a low power. Muscle fibers which run lengthwise immediately under the cuticle produce the energetic movements, and what appears to be a row of beads is the nucleus.

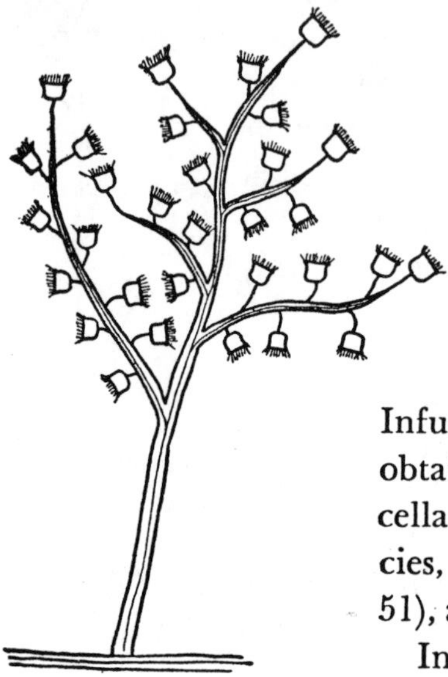

Two other species of Infusoria, which you should obtain by all means, are Vorticella (Figure 50), a solitary species, and Carchesium (Figure 51), a colonial form.

In both species, the animals are colorless, and bell-shaped in form, the front border of the body being surrounded with cilia, and they are, moreover, attached to a contractile stalk. In Vorticella each animal is fastened by its narrow part to a single stem, but in Carchesium the stem is divided at the summit into many branches, like a miniature tree, to which are attached a number of animals each with a short stem of its own. Both the unbranched stem of Vorticella and the branching stem of Carchesium have a muscular thread like a thin cord running through them, which can, with surprising suddenness, contract, pulling the single infusorium

FIGURE 51
Carchesium

Vorticella or the entire colony of Carchesium down to the point of attachment.

Vorticella and Carchesium are frequently referred to as flower animals, and I think you will agree when you view them, especially the Vorticellæ, for they will no doubt remind you of a bed of wee tulips, apparently growing out of a strand of green Algæ. If you watch them long enough you will suddenly see the stem of one of these "tulips" shorten and its "blossom" drop to the ground, to be followed by others. Then, as suddenly, you will see them slowly rise up again. The Vorticellæ are sometimes found in clusters of a hundred or more, and they are extremely amusing to watch as they bob up and down in a laughable manner. It is only when you see the stems straighten out that you will become aware of where the "blossoms" disappeared to.

ADVENTURE 24

We Learn the Use of Perfume

The use of perfumes and sweet smells by the members of the weaker sex as one of the blandishments with which to charm the unwary male is, I believe, as old as civilization itself, and it would not surprise me to learn some day that the distaff side of even our prehistoric ancestors had discovered the potency of fragrant odors.

Now it seems to me that every activity in which man

engages has its counterpart in the animal world. We build houses—so do many animals; we tunnel in the ground—so do the mining bees; we fly—so do the birds; we build roads and bridges—so do certain ants; we dairy—again so do ants; we sew—and still again, so do the tailor ants of India; we manufacture paper—so do the paper wasps; indeed, I could go on in this vein almost ad infinitum but these cases, which occur immediately to my mind, are sufficient, I think, to prove my point.

I began by speaking of our use of perfumes. This activity also finds its counterpart among the animals. I am thinking particularly of the butterflies—those beautiful and delicate creatures which an eminent American entomologist once termed the "frail children of the air." Years ago it was found that certain

FIGURE 52
Wing Scale

species appear to give off a distinct scent of pleasing fragrance, and later researches established the fact that scattered over the surface of the wings, or placed within certain special pockets, generally near the borders of the wings, are certain scales, called androconia, which give off an aromatic odor. In this day and age, we are inclined to look askance at any male that uses perfume or scent, but among the butterflies it is the males, and males only, that follow such a practice. So that instead of the female of the species seducing the male we have here the process completely reversed.

The androconia may easily be seen with the microscope. The white butterfly that is so commonly seen flying about our gardens is very well suited for our purpose. Examining the wing of one of these insects you will find that it is largely made up of scales such as shown in Figure 52. Mingled with these you will find some that appear as shown in Figure 53. These are the androconia.

FIGURE 53

Androconium

Another interesting feature of the butterflies is the manner in which they obtain nectar—the sweetish liquid which they obtain from flowers. As this liquid is secreted in nectaries which occur usually at the bases of the petals as swellings or as shallow cups, Nature has here again demonstrated how wondrous are her ways by providing the butterflies with the means for obtaining it. They are far too large in size to approach near enough to obtain it without some special device.

If we look closely at the head (Figure 54), we shall find extending from the lower part what appears to be a coiled spring. Indeed, if you take a pin and straighten it out and then release it, you will find that it will quickly

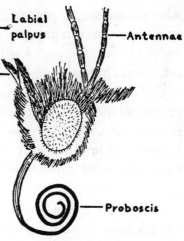

FIGURE 54

Butterfly Head

87

coil up again. This spring-like apparatus, called the proboscis, is nothing but a hollow tube fitted at one end (the end inside of the head) with a bulb. It serves as a sucking organ. In other words, the butterfly extends this sucking tube down into the flower to where the nectar is secreted and sucks up the sweet liquid much as you would use a "straw" in drinking your soda.*

ADVENTURE 25

We Test Our Morning Coffee

They say that the Swedes are the greatest coffee drinkers in the world and that they are the only people who know how to prepare really good coffee. I don't want to get into an argument on this point, for I am no judge of coffee, though I will admit that a cup of coffee sometimes hits the right spot.

Coffee is the seed of a small tree or shrub. In preparation for table use the coffee beans are subjected to roasting which changes the color of the bean to a rich brown, and in this form it is distributed to the retailer from whom we buy it and who, when we make our purchase, usually grinds it for us.

Frequently coffee is adulterated by a variety of substances such as peas and other legumes, cereal grains, starches, and chicory, to mention but a few, which are

* See Adventure 51 for further details about butterfly's mouth parts.

mixed in dough and then moulded to resemble the genuine roasted beans in form and color. Accordingly, whenever we buy coffee we do not know whether we are getting genuine coffee or adulterated coffee but we can very easily find out by a simple experiment. Merely throw a teaspoonful of the ground coffee onto the surface of some cold water. The genuine coffee, with the possible exception of a few highly roasted particles, will be found to float, while nearly all adulterants sink.

If you should find by such an experiment that you have received adulterated coffee, do not, in this instance, return it to the dealer as perhaps you would normally do, but instead why not learn, if possible, the nature of the adulterants which can only be determined by a microscopic examination. Perhaps I have "put my foot in it" by making such a suggestion, for obviously it is impossible within the narrow compass of this adventure for me to describe the appearance under the microscope of the various adulterants that are used. But I can show

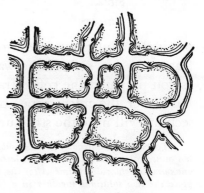

Figure 55
Coffee

you how to recognize the most commonly used adulterant—the root of the chickory plant.

First of all, we must see what coffee looks like. Take some of the ground coffee and place it on the surface of some cold water. Then select some of the larger fragments that float and with a razor blade cut some thin sections and place them in a solution of chlorinated soda * to remove some of the deep color. When the sections have been decolorized or bleached out, wash them in water and place them on a slide in a little diluted glycerine. They are now ready to be examined

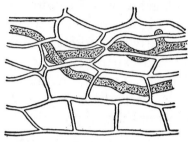

FIGURE 56

Chicory

and as we view them through the microscope we shall find that the coffee is made up of a network enclosing beaded or knotty thick-walled cells and filled with minute globules of oil (Figure 55).

To determine if chicory is the adulterant used, prepare some of the larger fragments that sink in the water in the same manner as you prepared the coffee fragments, and then examine under the microscope. If chicory is present, the sections will have the structure as shown in Figure 56.

* *To prepare chlorinated soda dissolve two ounces of washing soda in ten ounces of water. In another bottle place ten ounces of water and add one ounce of chloride of lime. After the chemicals are completely dissolved place the two solutions together in a larger container and let stand for several days. Then filter either through filter paper or through a finely woven fabric, when the preparation will be ready for use.*

We Learn Something about Sponges

Of course you know what Sponges are, or at least you think you do, but were I to ask you whether they are plants or animals what would your answer be? At one time they were considered plants, because of their irregular and plant-like habits of growth, but about 1857 scientists decided that they are animals. So the ordinary bath sponge that you use is an animal, or, more accurately, the skeleton of one.

The Sponges belong to a group called Porifera, from the Latin *porus,* a pore and *ferre,* to bear. Most of them live only in marine seas, but there are a few that inhabit fresh water. They have no powers of locomotion, but are attached to stones or plants along the shore or at depths up to 4000 fathoms. In form and shape they vary exceedingly, some being branched like trees, while others are fan-shaped, cup-shaped, or dome-shaped. They also vary markedly in size, some being no larger than a pinhead, while others are over five feet high. Most of them are white or gray, but there are many that are brilliantly colored and even iridescent, exhibiting all the colors of the rainbow.

A very simple Sponge, but one which will give you a pretty good idea of Sponges in general, is called Leucosolenia, which can be found growing on the rocks near the sea shore just below low-tide mark. It consists of a number of horizontal tubes from which branches extend up into the water. These branches are thin-walled sacs, with an opening called the osculum and with buds and branches projecting from their sides. The entire mass, as shown in Figure 57, is a colony of animals, and an individual Sponge is a single osculum and the tissues connected with it.

FIGURE 57
Leucosolenia

If you will examine an individual branch you will find it as pictured in Figure 58. Perhaps you might think that the osculum is the mouth, but in this you would be mistaken; on the contrary it is the anus. The cavity of the sac, called the gastral cavity, is a wide digestive cavity or "stomach" into which water bearing food enters through numerous small pores in the body-wall. On the inside walls of the cavity are located certain cells, called collar cells, each bearing a long whip-like process, the flagellum, such as is found on Euglena. The flagella beat constantly, creating a current of water which flows in the direction as shown by the arrows. If a living Sponge is placed in water and a little coloring matter added, you will be able to follow the course of the water

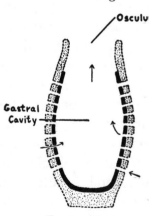

FIGURE 58
Individual Branch of Sponge

through the pores and up the cavity, finally flowing out through the osculum, over which is stretched a sieve-like membrane.

If you will again examine a branch, this time under the microscope, you will find that it contains a large number of three-pronged spicules (Figure 59). These spicules, composed of calcium carbonate, are embedded in the soft tissue of the body-wall and form the skeleton of the animal.* In other Sponges, the skeleton is made up of spicules of silicon, while in still others, it is made up not of spicules but of fibers

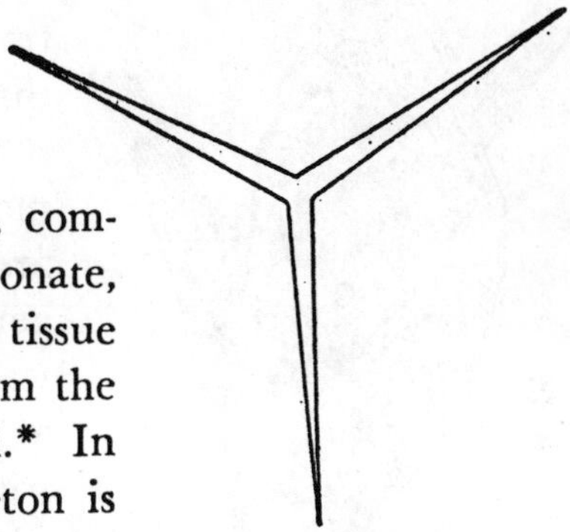

FIGURE 59
Sponge Spicule

of spongin, a substance which is chemically allied to silk, as in our common bath sponge.

Should you live too far from the sea shore to obtain Leucosolenia, you might look for the fresh water Sponge, Spongilla (Figure 60). It is gray or green in color and may be found attached to the under surface of rocks, dead leaves, or sticks, where it forms incrustations a fraction of an inch thick as compact masses. Scattered all over the surface are thousands of pores which lead into a network of canals and chambers which is somewhat more complicated than that of Leucosolenia. In this instance the water passes through

* *If you have difficulty in seeing the spicules, you may isolate them by boiling a bit of sponge in a five per cent solution of caustic potash for a few minutes.*

the pores, and, by way of incurrent canals, reaches a number of small chambers lined with flagella. From there it is in turn carried through an excurrent canal to the gastral cavity and finally out through the osculum.

Spongilla reproduces by means of gemmules, which are formed by a number of germinal cells in the body-wall and which gather into a ball and become surrounded by protecting spicules. They are formed in the autumn just before the death of the adult Sponge and live over the winter until spring when they develop into new Sponges, which first appear as tiny flecks of white upon submerged stones and twigs.

FIGURE 60
Spongilla

ADVENTURE 27

We Find Out What Chalk Is Made Of

On our ninth adventure, we learned that our toothpastes are sometimes composed of the skeletons of certain small plants called Diatoms. On our present adventure we are going to learn that white chalk is made up largely of the shells of tiny animals called Foraminifera.

The term foraminifera means having foramina or holes in the shell, this being the characteristic feature of these animals. There are more than two thousand kinds and most of them are marine, although there are a few fresh water forms. In size the average specimen is smaller than a pinhead and each individual consists of but a single cell of protoplasm, in which all the functions of life dwell. In this respect the Foraminifera remind us of the Amœbæ, and, as a matter of fact, are relatives of them.

The only essential difference between the Foraminifera and the Amœbæ is that the latter are devoid of a shell, undergo frequent changes in form, and have blunt pseudopodia, whereas the Foraminifera live within a shell, undergo no change in form, and have thread-like pseudopodia which issue through the foramina of the shell, or, where they are absent, through a single orifice. In this connection we might remark that they are strangely like Difflugia.

In the fresh-water forms, the shell is built of an organic substance which may be strengthened by silica or the incorporation of foreign particles. In those species that inhabit the marine seas the shells are composed of calcium carbonate with but the slightest trace of organic matter. When these shells sink to the sea bottom they become an ooze, which solidifies, forming a substance which we know as white chalk.

The Foraminifera reproduce as a rule by simple division, but in many cases simple division does not continue until complete separation into two individuals takes place, and in that event the new cells remain united to one another in a definite pattern, forming more or less ornate and small or large colonies. In this way thousands upon thousands of individuals may live in a colony, making calcareous structures sometimes as large as three inches across.

If you live near the sea shore you can find some of these interesting little animals in the ripples left by the tide. They may also be found at-

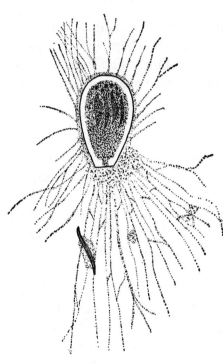

FIGURE 61
Allogramia

tached to underwater vegetation as seaweeds and also clinging to rocks and other forms of solid matter. Figure 61 shows a fresh-water species which goes by the name of Allogramia. You may have some difficulty in finding it, but it will repay your efforts with some very pleasant moments at the microscope.

ADVENTURE 28

We Inquire into the Nature of Yeast

If I were to ask you if you thought you knew what yeast is, you would probably look at me as if to say, what a ridiculous question. And if I were to ask you to tell me what it is, you would no doubt begin confidently, but I dare say that before long you would start er-er-erring and end up by lamely saying that yeast is the thing used in making bread.

Such an answer would be no more than I would expect, for surprisingly few people seem to know what it is, although everyone is familiar with it. So let us examine some of it and see what it is.

First of all we procure a yeast cake and mix one quarter of it with enough water to make a paste. Then we add one pint of water, with a tablespoonful of sugar, and stir well.

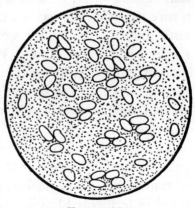

FIGURE 62
Yeast

We next place a drop of this cultural liquid on a slide and examine it under the highest power of the microscope. We shall find myriads of minute egg-shaped bodies (Figure 62). These bodies, of which the yeast cake is

97

almost wholly made up, are single one-celled plant organisms, individually known as yeast-plants.

These yeast-plants, like the other unicellular organisms that we have already met with, are units of protoplasm, enclosed within a well defined cell-wall (which can be brought out by adding a little glycerine or salt water) and containing a nucleus, oil globules, and vacuoles. Now we have seen that plants either make their own food (see Adventures 9-10-11) or obtain it parasitically from other plants (see Adventure 21). As we examine the yeast-plant we find no green bodies, so we conclude that chlorophyll must be lacking, and that therefore the plants must be parasites. Now this is not so, for they live, not on other living organisms, but instead on organic substances. This can be easily illustrated if we but turn to our cultural liquid. By now, bubbles of gas should be rising from the liquid. If we collect some of the gas and transfer it into a vessel containing limewater, we shall find that it becomes turbid, a sure sign that the gas is carbon dioxide. If we next taste some of the liquid we shall find that it is no longer sweet but alcoholic. What then has become of the sugar? The answer is that the yeast-plants have absorbed the sugar and by so doing disintegrated it into alcohol and carbon dioxide, a process which we know as fermentation.

This process of fermentation has wide economic use; indeed it is the basis of bread making, the manufacture of commercial ethyl alcohol, and the production of alcohol in fermented liquids used as beverages. So as the yeast-plants are the active agents of this process they are well-nigh indispensable to our well-being.

You have, no doubt, at some time or other, seen bread baked and at the time perhaps wondered what made the dough rise. The explanation, in view of what you have just learned, is very simple. In the first place, the yeast-plants are mixed with a mixture of flour and water. Now the flour contains a certain amount of sugar in addition to starch, and at a suitable temperature not only do the yeast-plants absorb the sugar but also multiply rapidly, the sugar meanwhile being broken down into alcohol and carbon dioxide. As the gas is formed, bubbles begin to permeate the dough and by their expansion cause it to rise, producing the sponginess peculiar to leavened bread. When the dough has raised sufficiently, it is placed in baking ovens, where there is a further expansion of bubbles and also a driving off of alcohol and water.

In the above paragraph I said something about the yeast-plants multiplying. This they do by a process called budding and is somewhat similar to the manner in which Hydra reproduces. When the yeast-plant is ready to reproduce, a bulging of the wall takes place. Into this dilatation or "bud" protoplasm flows, extending it still further until the one-celled yeast-plant consists of two unequal parts. Eventually, however, the connection between the two is severed, and the bud becomes detached from the original or parent cell. Sometimes the bud may give rise to buds of its own before it becomes detached and very often this budding may take place so rapidly that the connection may persist even during the formation of several generations of buds so that a number of cells may remain attached for a time in an irregular, fragile chain or colony.

The yeasts which are regularly employed in brewing and baking are usually termed "domesticated" or cultivated, to distinguish them from those in a state of nature. These "wild" yeasts, as they are sometimes referred to, are those which live in the sweet juices of plants or upon the surface of fruits, causing the latter, under certain circumstances, to ferment and decay. This is the reason why artificial ferments are not needed in making wine and other alcoholic liquors from fruits. If you examine a drop of sweet cider under the microscope you will find one of these species of wild yeasts.

ADVENTURE 29

We Go Microbe Hunting

In our last adventure we learned that yeast-plants are the active agents of fermentation. They are not, however, the only agents, for there are other organisms that also bring about fermentation, albeit a different kind of fermentation. These organisms are known as Bacteria.

Now we hear much about Bacteria, and why shouldn't we, for they are the most numerous of all living things. They are about us everywhere: in the air, in rain water, in freshly fallen snow, in all natural bodies of water, in the soil, in sewage—where they are particularly abundant—upon the surface of the human body, and for that matter upon the surface of all objects that have not recently been heated to a high temperature or otherwise sterilized, in the intestinal tract and on all the mucous membranes. Indeed, the only place where they appear not to exist is within the tissues of plants and animals, except when such organisms are suffering from one of the many diseases which they cause.

Since the Bacteria are so numerous and apparently not visible to the naked eye, they must obviously be very small in size; as a matter of fact they are the smallest known organisms, some of them being no more than .0005 millimeter in diameter, which is about the wave length of green light.

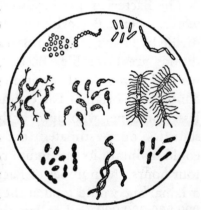

Not only are they the smallest known organisms but they are also the simplest. Typically they consist of but a single cell, which may have any one of a number of shapes as shown

FIGURE 63
Bacteria

in Figure 63. Usually they are classified into three principal types: spheres, rods and spirals, which are spoken of respectively as cocci, bacilli and spirilla, or in the singular as coccus, bacillus and spirillum.

When one looks at them for the first time they appear to be nothing more than pale and translucent bits of protoplasm. They possess, however, a cell wall, which does not ordinarily contain cellulose. The nucleus is not visible nor can you see any chlorophyll, for the simple reason that they do not possess any. They do not, therefore, manufacture their own food but live either on other animals or organic matter, digesting their food outside their bodies by the action of enzymes which they secrete. Some of them have the power of locomotion, being able to swim about in a liquid medium either by means of cilia, such as occur on Paramecium, or by flagella, such as occur on Euglena.

The Bacteria reproduce wholly by division. In other words, when a Bacterium attains its full growth it will divide by fission into two Bacteria of equal size. If conditions are favorable, Bacteria may increase by this method so rapidly that within a few hours the descendants of the original Bacterium may be literally countless. Someone, who apparently was inclined towards statistics, once estimated that if the cholera organism could maintain its maximum rate of fission for twenty-four hours, the number of Bacteria produced from the original one would total at the end of that time 1,600,000,000,000,000 and collectively would weigh almost half a million pounds!

In some kinds, the new cells separate immediately after division but in others they become embedded in a gelatinous matrix secreted by their walls, and in such cases remain attached in more or less fragile filaments or irregular masses. One such instance is the Bacteria which are responsible for the production of vinegar, the gelatinous mass being the so-called "mother of vinegar."

The Bacteria are probably best known as "germs" or "microbes" and thus looked upon in the popular mind as organisms of a baneful character. This is but natural in view of the prominence given to them as the causative agents of such human diseases as diphtheria, tuberculosis, cholera, pneumonia, typhoid and leprosy to name but a few, of such animal diseases as glanders, blackleg, anthrax, and chicken cholera, and of such plant diseases as fire blight of pears, wilt of egg plant, potato, cucumber and squash, and the soft rots of various vegetables. Bacteria are also harmful to man in that they cause the spoiling of food, while there are other forms that are associated with the decay of teeth.

On the other side of the ledger, the Bacteria have a number of good points. Indeed, great as the loss of life and property may be because of some of them, and widespread as the suffering for which some of them are responsible may be, many of them are instrumental in bringing about or promoting beneficial effects which no doubt far outweigh the harm which a few may do.

Perhaps the greatest single service which they render is the part they play in causing the decay of plant and animal bodies. Through this process such elements as carbon, oxygen, hydrogen, nitrogen, sulphur and phosphorus, which compose the bodies of plants and animals, are reduced to simple compounds such as water, nitrates, sulphates, phosphates and carbon dioxide, which can be used again as raw materials for food building in living plants. If it were not for these Bacteria and the process of decay, much of the available supply of certain essential elements would remain permanently tied up in the dead bodies of plants and animals with the result that what remained would not be enough to promote the growth and development of living plants and animals.

In addition to this service, certain Bacteria promote the fertility of the soil by taking the ammonia abundantly set free by decay Bacteria and transforming it into nitrates, while others absorb free nitrogen from the air and fix it in compounds utilizable by the higher plants, which are not able to use the free gas.

Bacteria are also essential to various industrial processes of great importance. As I said in the beginning, the Yeast-plants are not the only active agents of fermentation. However, the fermentation which certain Bacteria cause is not an alcoholic kind; on the contrary they oxidize various substances to organic acids,

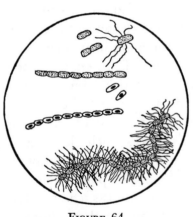

FIGURE 64
Hay Bacilli

thus producing a souring. The formation of vinegar is an example. Other processes in which the action of Bacteria is involved may be listed chiefly as follows: the tanning of leather; the preparation of flax fiber, used in the manufacture of linen cloth; the curing of tea; the manufacture of indigo; and the preservation of corn and other fodders in the form of ensilage, and of cabbage as sauerkraut. Finally, there are some which produce the special flavors and odors in ripening cheeses, while still others are concerned in the ripening of stored tobacco.

As plentiful and as common as Bacteria may be, they are not always easy to capture just when you want them. However, we can obtain some of them without much difficulty by merely putting some hay in water and leaving it in a warm place away from the light until the liquid becomes cloudy or a film forms on the surface. If we now examine a drop of this liquid under the microscope we shall find it swarming with Bacteria, a majority of which are the Hay Bacilli (Figure 64). In their active state these organisms consist of single-celled, rod-shaped bodies, about three or four times as long as broad, and generally cohering in bands or filaments. The black dots within the cells are the spores. You will notice that some forms move about freely, while others remain stationary, the motion being either mechanical like the movement of dust particles dancing about in the sunshine, or voluntary and produced by the vibration of the cilia.

Should we let the liquid stand a day or two longer after first examining it with the microscope, we shall find numerous infusoria in addition to the Bacteria. If you remember, I mentioned in Adventure 23 that infusoria were so-named because they were first discovered in infusions. Accordingly, the culture which we have just prepared is known as a hay infusion because the principal constituent used was hay.

Another method of obtaining Bacteria is to take several tablespoonfuls of beefsteak broth and mix it with a small quantity, say a thimbleful, of gelatin and a pinch of baking soda. The mixture is then boiled until the gelatin has melted, when it is placed in a dish and left exposed for an hour or so in an ordinary room. We then remove the dish and its contents to a warm place where we leave it for a few days. Then we shall find that a number of spots of different colors will have developed on the surface of the culture medium. If we now take samples of these spots and examine them on a slide under the microscope, using the highest power of objective that we have, we shall perhaps find that most of them are fungus growths. Some of them, however, should be thriving colonies of Bacteria. Should we see nothing at all, it is simply because the Bacteria are too small to be seen with the objective that we have at our disposal.

For the proper microscopical examination of such Bacteria as we may obtain by either method, it is necessary to subject them to certain treatment. Our procedure consists first in removing a specimen from the culture medium to a slide upon which we pour a few drops of alcohol, which we ignite immediately with a match. This is to kill and fix the Bacteria. Next we add a drop of methylene blue, and when it is completely soaked in, we wash the excess off with water. If we are anxious to proceed with our examination, we may drive off the moisture quickly by passing the slide gently back and forth over a low flame, otherwise we may put it aside to dry of its own accord. In either case, when the stained spot is dry, we add a drop of Canada balsam and over the whole place a cover glass. Our specimen is now ready and so we transfer it to the stage of the microscope and proceed with our examination.

We Perform a Spicy Experiment

In some of the preceding adventures, we have examined a number of common foods which are frequently adulterated. Spices are not exactly foods, perhaps, but they are widely used, nevertheless, to make foods more palatable. And they, too, are frequently adulterated.

Now it is impossible for us to examine all of the spices to be found in the average household, so we shall confine ourselves to those most generally used, namely mustard and pepper.

If we take some powdered mustard, place it on a slide in a drop of water and examine it under the microscope, we shall find it to have the structure as shown

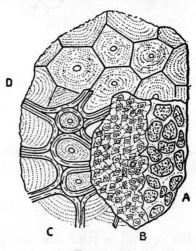

FIGURE 65
Structure of Mustard

in Figure 65. In a good table mustard the bulk of the sample should be made up of the structure designated by A. If an excess of B, C and D are present, we have evidence that mustard-hulls have been added, and this is one of the common adulterations. Sometimes wheat and rice starch are added and we should also look for the characteristic grains of both of these starches (See Adventure 17).

So much for mustard, and we next turn our attention to pepper, which is the pulverized seed of a shrub cultivated mainly in the East Indian islands. The dried seed is about five millimeters in diameter and is covered with a brownish hull. If this hull is ground up with the grain, there results the ordinary black pepper, whereas white pepper is made by macerating the fruit in water before drying, and detaching the hulls by friction.

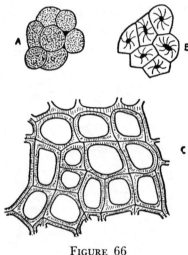

FIGURE 66
Structure of Pepper

If we examine some ground black pepper, we shall find a number of tissues, since the hulls are relatively thick as compared with the central portion and are made up of a number of layers. The central portion, which forms the bulk of the preparation, is quite characteristic in appearance and consists of irregularly angular whitish masses, made up of polygonal cells containing very minute starch grains, as shown by A in Figure 66. In addition to these starch masses we should find at least two characteristic kinds of cells from the hull, and these are shown by B and C. As white pepper is made up simply of the central part of the seed, we should find, on examining a sample, practically nothing but the silvery masses of pepper starch (A).

As pepper is one of the commonly adulterated spices and may be mixed with a wide variety of substances, all that we can do is to determine the presence of any substance other than the normal tissues of the pepper. Of course, should we be expert food analysts, we might be able to determine the nature of the adulterant, but then only by careful comparison with a series of known pure substances.

ADVENTURE 31

We Dig for Worms

Have you ever noticed that the mud on the bottom of your favorite pond or pool sometimes appears to be tinged with a reddish color? If you will gather some of this mud and examine it, you will find that the color is due to a small worm. Now this worm is in itself colorless and transparent, but it possesses bright crimson blood, which gives it such a vivid hue that when it is numerous the mud in which it lives appears as if colored.

This little worm, known as Tubifex (Figure 67), is thread-like in form and measures from one-half to one and one-half inches in length. It is rarely found free-swimming but lives in a tube, which it builds, with its tail sticking up above the surface of the sur-

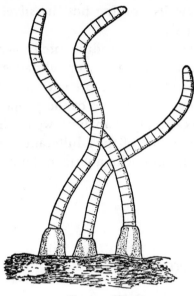

FIGURE 67
Tubifex

rounding mud. The tail is in constant motion, waving to and fro beyond the edge of the tube.

It feeds on decaying organic matter, which it obtains by digging its head an inch or more down into the bottom mud, and all waste matter from the body is ejected from the tail projecting beyond the tube. Thus Tubifex behaves much like the earthworm, overturning the ooze of pond bottoms as the earthworm overturns the topsoil of the land.

Tubifex belongs to the same group as the earthworm, and if you know anything about zoology you will know that, like the earthworm, it is divided into segments or rings, which are apparent on the outside by clearly defined constrictions. On each segment there is one or more comparatively short, fine, hair-like bristles which appear to be arranged in a single row on each side of the body. There is also an additional row of stouter, inflexible, gracefully curved spines, which in other worms are used in locomotion and thus known as foot spines. As they are retractile you may not find them very easily and in that case it might be necessary

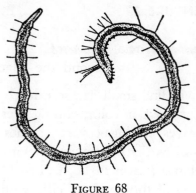

FIGURE 68

Nais

to compress the worm between the slide and the cover glass before they will become conspicuous. Then you will notice that they seem to be but slightly curved and somewhat forked.

There are a number of other aquatic worms with bristles so conspicuous that they have been called bristleworms. Such a species is Nais (Figure 68) which is very common in the mud or among Algæ or on the leaflets of various water plants. It is whitish or yellowish in color and is free-swimming, moving about with the aid of foot spines and bristles, the bristles near the front end usually being the longest. Another species is Dero (Figure 69), which measures hardly a quarter of an inch long, and with a posterior extremity that is broad and funnel-like. It is common on floating plants, but sometimes it buries itself in the mud with the posterior end protruded from a small mud chimney which it may build.

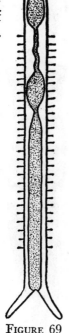

FIGURE 69

Dero

We Meet Some More Worms

Quite commonly you will find small flat, soft, leech-like animals, either gray or black in color, gliding over submerged stems and leaves or Alga-covered stones. These creatures are known as Flatworms, and belong to a group called Turbellaria (Latin *turbo,* I disturb) from the turbulent lashing of thousands of cilia with which they are covered and to which they owe their

motion. The cilia are visible only under a high power but you can see the result of their motion with a one inch objective, as they create currents in the water that sweep away small objects with considerable rapidity.

The Turbellarians are generally abundant in fresh water and can be found at any time of the year. Most of these worms are visible to the naked eye as small whitish threads, but there are two forms which are quite large in comparison with them. These are the leech-like creatures mentioned above. One of them is velvety black in color, with a slender body, tapering into a pointed tail and with a head broader than the body, and measuring about one quarter of an inch in length. It is one of the most common Flatworms and is known by the name of Planaria

FIGURE 70
Planaria

(Figure 70). The other form is known as Dendrocœlum (Figure 71). It is somewhat smaller in size and creamy white in color, altogether a most beautiful little animal. If possible try to obtain this form, for its internal anatomy is more easily made out than that of Planaria,

FIGURE 71
Dendrocœlum

as the latter is usually so full of coloring matter that hardly anything is visible.

These two Flatworms, frequently spoken of as Planarians, seem to prefer shallow ponds and streams, where they may be found crawling over stones, submerged logs, and water plants. They are carnivorous in

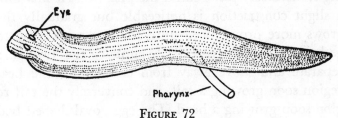

FIGURE 72
Planaria with Protruded Pharynx

habit, seeming to prefer Rotifers and Infusoria. The mouth is on the end of a short muscular tube called the pharynx, which is located in the middle of the body and which can be protruded or withdrawn at will through a small opening on the under side (Figure 72).

When a Planarian feeds, the pharynx is thrust well out of the body and then moved about like a feeler or proboscis until it comes in contact with the food, which is then sucked through it. From the pharynx the food passes into a branching intestine, which in Dendrocœlum may be seen as a vinelike tracery of brown. As the Flatworms have no anal opening, undigested material must be ejected through the mouth; and frequently one may see one of these Planarians vomit up a mass of undigested and empty shells and other body coverings, as well as many unrecognizable particles and fragments.

On the upper surface near the front end, there is a pair of small blackish or reddish eye-spots. The Planarians seem to be very sensitive to the conditions of their environment, particularly temperature and bright light, which they always try to avoid.

They reproduce both by division and eggs, dividing transversely just behind the pharynx. At first only a slight constriction is noticeable but gradually this grows more pronounced until the two parts hang together by a mere thread. Eventually the two parts separate and move away from each other, the head region soon growing a tail, and conversely the tail region soon growing a head. The eggs, oval-shaped bodies, are usually dropped anywhere in the mud or the water.

The Planarians have great powers of regeneration. As I just said they normally reproduce by dividing transversely; each part grows a complete new animal. But if one should be cut lengthwise through the center of the body, the right side will regenerate a new left and vice versa. The head alone will grow into an entire animal. As a matter of fact, pieces cut from various parts of the body will also regenerate completely. Pieces from one animal may also be grafted upon another, and in this way many curious and strange-looking monsters have been produced.

ADVENTURE 33

We Receive a Pleasant Surprise

Nature's object in hiding some of her most beautiful creations from the eyes of man seemingly can only be explained away by putting it down to a whim, for what could her motive otherwise have been? I am thinking of the Bryozoa, minute animals of such an exquisite and delicate beauty that Nature must have been in a happy mood when she fashioned them. Perhaps Nature wanted to reserve for herself and her devotees delights that come from an appreciation of the beautiful, and so made them imperceptible to the vulgar; for though they are most abundant in our slow moving streams and shallow ponds, only those who have become Nature's disciples and have been initiated into her mysteries know what they look like or where to find them.

The Bryozoa, sometimes called moss animals from their similarity to moss, usually live in colonies which are always attached to some submerged object. The

FIGURE 73
Plumatella

colonies are visible to the naked eye, some of them being quite conspicuous, but the individual animals are too minute to be seen except with a hand lens. In some species such as Plumatella (Figure 73), the colonies are formed of narrow brownish sheaths or tubes secreted by the animals, which adhere to the lower surface of waterlogged sticks or lily pads or the submerged stems of grasses, where they branch like miniature trees.

In other forms such as Pectinatella (Figure 74), the colonies or communities are surrounded by a thick rather firm jelly-like material. These jelly masses, usually colorless and semi-transparent, though sometimes tinged a pale red, are about the size of a marble and may be found attached to almost any submerged object, even to smooth stones. Within such protective coverings the little animals live. When undisturbed they project a part of their body beyond the orifice of the tubes or from pores in the surrounding jelly, but when frightened or dis-

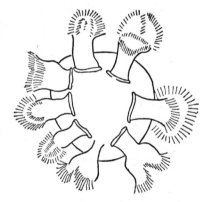

FIGURE 74
Pectinatella

116

turbed quickly retreat and leave no sign of life behind them.

When collecting the Bryozoa, the tubular or jelly-like colonies appear lifeless and altogether unattractive and you may think that they are not worth looking at. But I can assure you that you are in for a pleasant surprise.

In order to examine them under the microscope it is necessary to use a rather deep life slide to hold the large quantity of water that they require. Another requisite is to keep the water perfectly quiet, as the slightest disturbance will terrify the timid animals, whereupon they will remain within their protective coverings. But if you will follow these two requirements and exercise a little patience all will go well.

At first you will see nothing but the surface of the jelly or the tips of the branching tube, depending on what species you have obtained. But after a while, a little projection appears within the field of vision and slowly lengthens and broadens, retreating and reappearing a number of times until finally, after seeming to hesitate, it suddenly bursts into bloom, its narrow body lifting above the jelly or tube a circular or horseshoe wreath, ornamented with long tentacles that seem as fine as hairs and which sparkle and glisten as they move and twist about. As you are held spellbound by this lovely vision, another and still another spreads its wreath and moves its tentacles, until the whole surface of the jelly-mass or branching tubes are abloom like a garden of fairyland.

You seem suddenly transported to a land of enchantment and you watch in silent admiration at the scene unfolded before you. And then, unaware of a quickening pulse and the feeling of excitement stealing over you, you perhaps jar the water ever so slightly, when, in a twinkling of the eye, all will have disappeared, as if you had seen a fleeting vision of another world. But this fleeting vision you can recapture, and if you remain quiet and motionless the enchanted garden will reappear, and all will be as beautiful and as lovely as before.

The wreath of tentacles—the head of the animal—is called the lophophore, in the center of which is the mouth. Each tentacle is covered with cilia, as the microscope will show, and these wave toward the mouth, whirling along such microscopic organisms that serve as food. From the mouth, a food passage or œsophagus extends to the stomach, which is a widened tube. This is followed by a tubular intestine which curves forward and opens either just inside or just outside the circlet of tentacles. Through it the undigested food material is ejected. The body is a transparent membranous sack with the lophophore at the free end, and the remainder immersed in the jelly or hidden in the sheath or tube, and provided with muscles by which the animal can pull itself together. Thus, when frightened, the sides of the lophophore close together, the tentacles collect themselves into a bundle, and the whole front is drawn back into the body, a muscle around the border then closing the opening. The jelly or tubes are therefore the protection afforded the body, while the body in turn receives and encloses the lophophore and tentacles. When all danger is past, the bundle of tentacles is cautiously pushed forward, followed by the lophophore, and if all seems safe, the tentacles are spread open, revealing the animal in all its beauty and grace.

Upon the approach of cold weather in the fall, cold-resistant winter buds called statoblasts are formed within the body. They are similar to the gemmules of the sponge

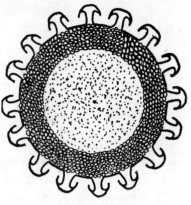

FIGURE 75
Statoblast of Pectinatella

Spongilla and are set free in the water after the animal has died and its protective covering broken into pieces. Some statoblasts, as those of Pectinatella for instance, are enclosed in tough cushions which buoy them up like life preservers and are armed with hooks which anchor them to twigs and other floating objects (Figure 75).

ADVENTURE 34

We Examine a Moss Plant

In our last adventure I remarked that the Bryozoa were sometimes called moss-animals from their similarity to moss. Now we all know what moss is—the green mat-like or tussock-like masses which grow not

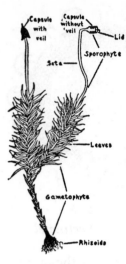

FIGURE 76

Moss Plant

only on the ground but also on fallen tree trunks and fences and other similar places. But few of us have examined such plants and really know what they look like. There are many species of mosses, but a group that is especially suited for our study, because the various species that comprise it are so large that the individual parts can be easily made out, is that which is known as the Hairy-caps. These are, also, the most common mosses and may be found bordering wood-trails and wood-roads or covering the ground in almost all open places.

An individual moss plant or gametophyte, appears as shown in Figure 76 and consists of a vertical slender stem, bearing spirally-arranged, very thin, small green leaves, with a long-stalked spore capsule rising above it in the air. It is anchored to the ground by rather stout root-like hairs (rhizoids). As compared to the higher plants, both leaves and stems are simple in structure, the various cell layers being not greatly differentiated from one another.

The most striking part of the plant is perhaps the fruity portion, called the sporophyte, and its various parts (Figure 76). The spore case, within which are contained myriads of green dust-like spores, is a thin-walled cylindrical box or capsule borne on a flexible stalk (seta) and in certain stages covered with a conical

120

light-brown hairy cap or veil (Figure 76). When this veil or cap falls off, the case is found to be tightly shut by a round lid, the edges of which fit closely about the rim of the spore-case.

As the spores of the Hairy-cap mature, the stalk bends so as to bring the spore case in a horizontal position. The lid, pushed up by the swelling of a ring of short bead-like cells, now falls off, revealing a number

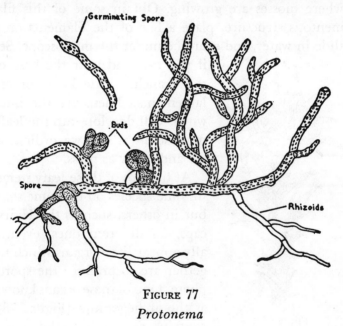

FIGURE 77
Protonema

of blunt teeth bordering the rim of the case and bending inward. These bear at their extremities a thin membranous disk which closes the case. These teeth are hygroscopic in nature and react according to the weather. When the weather is damp they hold the membranous disk so that the spores cannot escape, but when it is dry they become so modified as to form a ring of holes between the teeth and the edge of the disk through which the spores may pass.

The spores are disseminated by the wind and on finding a suitable place they germinate into a branching, filamentous, creeping green structure called Protonema (Figure 77), which spreads over the ground and forms the tangled green felt sometimes observed where mosses are growing. Obtain some of this filamentous structure, place a few of the filaments on a slide in water, and examine under the microscope. See

FIGURE 78
Archegonium in Section

if you can find near the base of the branches little knots or enlargements. These are the buds which will develop into the leafy moss stems which we ordinarily see and know as moss.

At the tips of these leafy stems, in some species on the same stem but in others, such as the Hairy-caps, on different ones, eventually appear little organs which together are to produce the sporophyte. One of these organs known as the archegonium (Figure 78), contains an egg-cell; the other, known as the antheridium (Figure 79), contains two tailed, spiral free-swimming sperm or fertilizing cells, which probably reach the archegonium in splashing water drops.

However the sperm cells may reach the archegonium, the fact remains that they do, the first one reaching it effecting fertilization of the egg-cell. Upon the union of these two cells, a division of the egg-cell takes place and this is followed by a multiplication of cells, the ultimate result of which is a mass of tissue called a sporogonium. This is the fruit of the moss plant, and as it grows within the archegonium the wall of the

FIGURE 79
Antheridium in Section

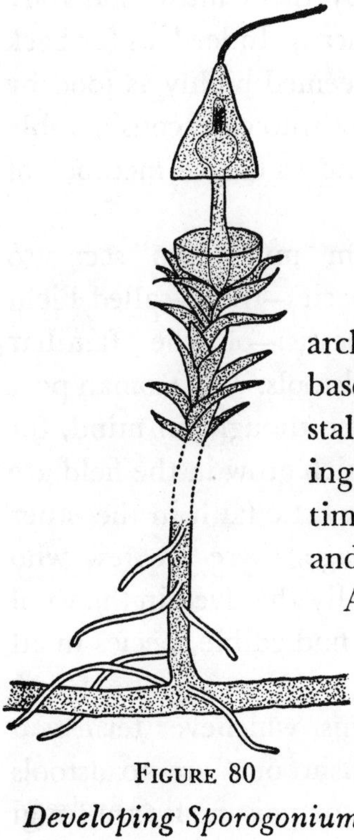

archegonium is torn away at the base and is carried up on the stalk as a cap or veil on the growing sporogonium (Figure 80). In time the spores ripen and escape and the process is repeated.

Although mosses have no great economic value, they have a place in the economy of Nature by their ability to retain great quantities of water in their spongy masses

FIGURE 80
Developing Sporogonium

and thus often prevent violent and excessive torrents of water from pouring down mountainsides into the valleys below.

We Make a Study of Toadstools

I do not know whether you like mushrooms but a great many people do, and by them mushrooms are considered something of a delicacy. Indeed, as far back as ancient times they were esteemed highly as food by the Greek and Roman epicures who gave considerable thought to their cultivation and to choice methods of preparing them for the table.

In the popular mind the term "mushroom" seems to be limited to a single edible species—the so-called Field Mushroom (Agaricus Campestis)—of the familiar growths which we know as toadstools. The Roman poet Horace must have had the same thought in mind, for he says that the mushrooms which grow in the field are the best and that one can have little faith in the other kinds. In this "enlightened" age, there are few who would agree with him, especially the dyed-in-the-wool mushroom eaters who seem to find edible species in all sorts of imaginable places.

The toadstools or mushrooms, whichever term you prefer, for botanically all mushrooms are toadstools and vice versa, whether edible or poisonous, are fungi which, as we learned in Adventure 21, are plants containing no chlorophyll and therefore incapable of supporting a separate existence. In other words, as they can manufacture no food they must consequently obtain it ready-made from the tissues of living or dead animals and plants. The toadstools feed for the most

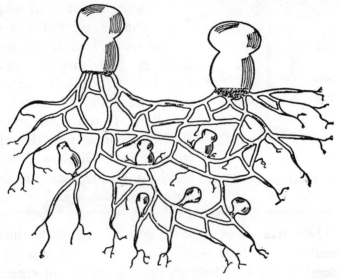

FIGURE 81
Mushroom Mycelium

part, not on living tissues, but on dead organic substances, obtaining their food by means of a network of fine threads called the mycelium. But let us start at the beginning and trace the life history of these unusual plants and consider in turn the different structures as we come to them.

The toadstools reproduce by spores. These consist

of but a single cell, are microscopic in size, and are scattered by the wind. On finding favorable soil they germinate, that is, the spores or cells begin to absorb food through the cell walls and after a while divide into two cells. In turn each of these cells divide and so the process is continued until long chains of cells are formed which look to the unaided eye like threads. Each one of these threads is called a hypha and a tangle of them is a mycelium. If you place some of this mycelium under the microscope you will observe that the threads or hyphæ are made up of cells placed end to end as in Spirogyra * (Figure 81).

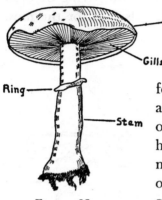

Figure 82

Mushroom

These threads or hyphæ interlace with each other and frequently form webby mats that ramify to a considerable distance through the substratum of rotton wood or other material upon which the plant grows. This webby structure or mycelium is often mistaken for root fibers, but, on the contrary, it is the vegetative body of the plant, the part rising above the ground, usually considered as the mushroom or toadstool, being the fruit, or reproductive organ.

* As the toadstools are quite common you should not have any difficulty in obtaining such plants, but in collecting them be sure to obtain a portion of the substratum on which they grow, containing some of the so-called spawn or mycelium. If unable to obtain any of the toadstools, the common mushroom sold in the market will do very well.

While examining the mycelium see if you can find any small round bodies. These are called buttons and are formed of the threads matting together. No larger than a pinhead at first, they soon increase in size and as they grow a minute stem appears, which gradually lifts

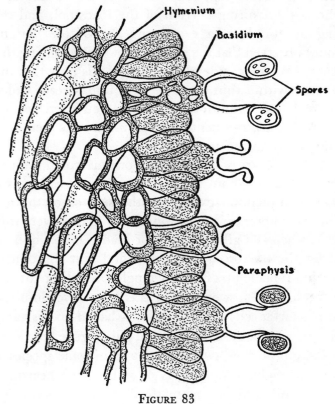

FIGURE 83
Section of Mushroom Gill

the button above the soil where it expands into a mature mushroom or toadstool.

As toadstools are common enough, you are naturally

more or less familiar with their appearance. A representative type is shown in Figure 82 and consists of the following parts: the handle, known as the stem; the open top, known as the cap; the gills, which are the thin plates under the cap radiating from the stem to the edge of the cap, somewhat like the spokes of a wheel—the fruiting portion of the toadstool; and the ring or annulus. In examining the button you no doubt observed that the gills are not visible during this stage of the plant's development. At this time they are covered with a thin sheet of mycelium threads called the veil. As the button grows, this veil stretches and finally breaks, frequently remaining on the stem as a ring known as the annulus.

The structure of the toadstool or mushroom is much the same throughout the entire plant—consisting as it does of mycelium—except on the surface of the gill where a difference is to be found. If you cut a very thin section across a gill with a razor blade and examine it under the microscope, you will find that the central portion is made up of loosely tangled mycelium threads or hyphæ and just outside of this loose mycelium layers of shorter cells which bear club-shaped bodies standing out over both surfaces of the gill (Figure 83). Some of these bear from two to four, and in some species as many as eight, little prongs or stalks, each bearing a spore, while others remain sterile. The spore-bearing cells are called basidia,* the sterile ones, paraphyses; and the entire spore-bearing surface the hymenium, from the Greek word meaning a membrane.

* *The toadstools belong to a group of plants called Basidiomycetes, so called from the basidium, plural basidia.*

In spite of the fact that most toadstools are edible, most people shy away from them, probably because of the fatal results produced by some of them, as the deadly amanita and the equally dangerous fly mushroom. A great many people also shy away from them because of the damp and gruesome places where many of them flourish. And I suppose I can't blame them overly much. But I cannot wholly agree with Shelly who wrote:

> *"And agarics and fungi, with mildew and mould,*
> *Started like mist from the wet ground cold;*
> *Pale, fleshy, as if the decaying dead*
> *With a spirit of growth had been animated."*

or with Spenser who penned:

> *"The grisly todestool grown there mought I see,*
> *And loathed paddocks (toads) lording on the same."*

For toadstools are not altogether noxious; indeed, quite the contrary. There are many which in their bright coloring and exquisite symmetry of form are quite pleasing to the eye. I refer to such forms as the beautiful white Bear's Head, hanging stately on tree trunks, or the Death Cup, gleaming white on the ground, or the beautiful green or red Russulas, or the brilliant golden Clavarias, or the dainty Oreades which cause fairy rings to grow on lawns and hillsides.

Economically the toadstools and their kin, such as the puffballs, shelf fungi and earth-stars, are the cause of considerable loss to the forester as they are responsible for much wood decay, destroying millions of feet of lumber each year. As an article in our dietary, while serving as a pleasant relish, their food value has been greatly exaggerated, inasmuch as they contain too large a percentage of water, sometimes over 90 per cent. As a matter of fact, the most highly prized of them all, the common mushroom sold in the market, in nutrient properties, is about equivalent to the cabbage.

ADVENTURE 36

We Become Farmers

We are all familiar with the peculiar growths that frequently appear, to our dismay, on bread, preserves, fruit and other foods, and which we know as molds. Usually we try to prevent the formation of such growth but for once we are intentionally going to promote their formation. All we need to do is to take a piece of moistened bread, cover it with an inverted tumbler and place it in a fairly warm place. A day or two later a delicate fuzzy growth of a white, green or black color will appear on its surface.

If we now take some of this growth and examine it under the microscope, we will find it to consist of innumerable delicate threads which branch or ramify so profusely over the substratum as to present often a woolly or cobwebby appearance (Figure 84). These threads look strangely similar to those which we found in the toadstools and are, as a matter of fact, analogous to them, being the mycelium or the vegetative body of the growth, which is also, like the toadstool, a fungus, since it does not manufacture its own food but derives it from organic substances.

At various places on the mycelium you will find tall vertical stalks, called hyphæ, rising into the air, on which are borne small spheres which at first are white but later turn black, forming the distinctive black spots of the Bread Mold (Figure 84).

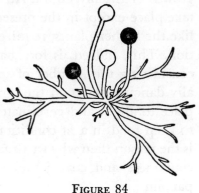

FIGURE 84
Bread Mold

These spheres contain spores numbering a hundred or more, which when mature break out of the walls of the spheres and are scattered into the air. Here they might live a considerable time, since they possess stored food, until they become deposited on favorable material, when they germinate and form hyphæ, from which an entire new mycelium similar to the one from which they came will develop.

On examining the threads of the mycelium under the microscope you will find that each is bounded by a thin wall and filled with a granular semi-liquid substance containing various clear spaces and denser particles. This substance, I think, you will recognize as protoplasm. Through the mycelium, foods in solution and various salts containing the elements necessary for the continued life of the protoplasm are absorbed from the bread or whatever substratum the mold is growing on, and in turn are broken down, with the formation of new protoplasm, and new cells, resulting in the growth of the mycelium. All of this, however, cannot take place except in the presence of air, for the molds, like the higher plants, require free oxygen for respiration. This, indeed, is fortunate for us, for otherwise, considering the number of spores which are continually dancing about in the air looking for a favorable place to alight and germinate, we would be hard put to keep food in a fit condition for consumption. This is the reason then why we usually keep food in air-tight containers and coat jellies and jams with layers of paraffin.

The species of mold which we have just cultivated and examined belongs to a group called the Black Molds. Most of the members of this group, like Bread Mold, obtain their food from non-living material, but there are some which are parasitic, deriving their food from the bodies of living organisms. One of these, known as Empusa muscorum, kills the common House Fly. The spore germinates on the body of the insect and the hypha penetrates the tissues, becoming a mycelium, which causes a diseased condition that usually ends in death. Perhaps you have often seen a dead fly surrounded by a halo of whitish dust. This dust is the sporangia shot from the hyphae of the fungus. If you wish proof of what I say, examine some of this dust under the microscope the next time you find a fly in such a condition and see for yourself.

In addition to this group there is another group of molds known as the Blue and Green Molds. Superficially, these molds resemble the Black Molds but there are some differences, most prominent being the bluish or greenish, instead of blackish, spore masses. There are some two hundred and fifty species of them and though they frequently occur among the Black Molds, they extend more widely than they, occurring in almost all kinds of damp organic bodies, such as cheese, leather, wall paper—in fact on almost anything that will "mold" in dampness.

We View the Most Primitive Insects

On the surface of still pools, and sometimes on the snow during bright spring days, tiny dark specks may be seen which, when disturbed, appear to spring about like so many jumping-jacks. These minute creatures are insects and are called Spring-tails. Now most things are named from some characteristic feature; and so if we assume the rule to hold good in this instance, we should gather that these insects have a tail which serves as some sort of a spring. That is true, and if you will examine one of these Spring-tails you will

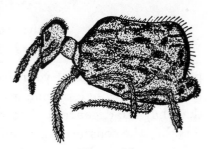

FIGURE 85
Spring-tail

133

find located on the underside of the abdomen a spring-like process which, when the insect is at rest, is held under the abdomen but when straightened out propels it into the air.

Viewing a Spring-tail under the low power of the microscope you will find it to be a most grotesque, looking creature (Figure 85). But more than that you will be looking at what is considered to be one of the simplest forms of insect life, for the Spring-tails have no wings, and for that matter never have had any, and in their development do not pass through the successive stages that the other insects do. From new-born to adult they grow up without as much change as takes

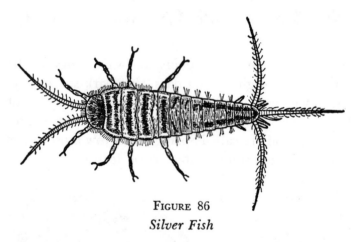

FIGURE 86
Silver Fish

place in the growth of your dog or cat. From the fact that they are wingless some investigators have believed that they are degenerate descendants of winged ancestors, but the consensus of opinion now is that they are primitively wingless insects; in other words that they originated before insects acquired wings.

Though the Spring-tail lacks many of the specialized structures and the more highly developed parts to be found in other insects, it is not the most primitive insect we can meet with. This honor, if honor it can be called, goes to the small, wingless, carrot-shaped, silver-shining creature (Figure 86) commonly known as the Silver fish, or Fish-moth, or Bristle-tail, so often a very troublesome household enemy of books, papers, starched clothing, and sometimes stored foods. I am not going to suggest that you capture and examine one of these animals, for to do so might convey the impression that I am hinting that your household might be a haven for "undesirables" of this kind and perhaps others. But such "undesirables" do sometimes get into the best regulated families.

If by chance you should ever examine one of these insects under the microscope you will find it to be a very pretty little creature indeed, covered as it is with scales usually of a silvery appearance. It is carrot-shaped in form and has three long antenna-like processes issuing from the end of the abdomen. These processes are called cerci and are tactile in function.

The Bristle-tail is a more primitive insect than the Spring-tail as it is simpler in structure. This is shown by the absence of any specialized structure such as the springing organ of the Spring-tail.

The Bristle-tails move about very rapidly and as they abhor light, they make active efforts to conceal themselves. If you try to catch them you will find that they are very elusive, and slip through the fingers with ease, leaving them covered with their scales which they cast off to facilitate their escape.

There are a number of species of these Bristle-tails, most of which are to be found among books, papers, starched clothing and other articles of a similar nature. There is one species, however, that seems to prefer the vicinity of fireplaces, and similar spots, sometimes being abundant in bake shops, running over the hot stones with utter disregard for the effects of high temperatures, and called in consequence the Fire-brat.

ADVENTURE 38

We Learn to Distinguish Textile Fibers

The weaving of plant or animal fibers into fabrics for clothing or other purposes is as old as civilization, but how different are the processes employed today as compared to the crude methods followed by our forefathers, to say nothing of those in vogue at the time of the ancients. Compare an old-fashioned hand loom with a giant loom, such as is to be found in our textile mills, and you will have an illustration of what miracles human ingenuity can perform. To be sure such a miracle is but one of many which have been performed during the last hundred years and only the future will reveal what others are in store for us. The development of chemical science, which has been so rapid in the last few years, will, if present indications hold good, produce synthetic products and materials that will be as revolutionary as the mechanical inventions of the past century. As a case in point, I might refer you to the synthetic fibers which are becoming the vogue and which will take their place with those natural fibers that have so long been used.

Now the microscopic examination of fibers has long been employed by the textile industry to determine the quality of fibers before they are woven into fabrics, and by buyers of the finished products for the purpose

FIGURE 87
Cotton

of detecting fraud. I am sure you will want to know how to recognize the various fibers used in textiles and to be able to tell if the handkerchief you are using is pure linen or if the suit or dress you are wearing is "all wool" or partly cotton. So let us get to work.

The first fiber that we shall examine is cotton, the most important of the vegetable fibers. Cotton consists of the hairs that cover the seeds of various species of Gossypium. These hairs are separated from the seeds by machinery, and, after passing through various processes, are spun into yarn. Obtain, if possible, a little raw cotton, or failing that, a little ordinary nonabsorbent cotton wool. Take a few threads, moisten them with a drop of alcohol on a slide and allow most of the alcohol to evaporate. Then add a drop of water, cover with a cover glass, and examine under the high power.

On doing so you will find that the hairs some-what resemble twisted ribbon (Figure 87), the edges of which are considerably thickened. Running up the center, there is a narrow cavity or lumen, as it is called. Covering the whole there is a skin or cuticle which is sometimes lacking in the fibers of cotton fabric owing to the chemicals with which the raw cotton has been treated.

The next fiber that we shall examine is that of flax which is used in the manufacture of linen. Flax consists of the bast fibers from the stem of the flax plant, which are separated from the plant by various processes. If possible, procure from a rope maker a little

FIGURE 88
Flax

raw flax. Failing this, pull out some threads of a fabric which you know certainly to be linen. In the latter case shred the threads apart with the points of large needles until you have the individual fibers separated. From whichever source you procure the fibers, place them in a drop of water on a slide, cover with a cover glass, and examine under the microscope. You will find that the fibers have very thick walls (Figure 88), with a lumen that is narrow and uniform in width and containing a little granular matter. On the walls you may detect delicate oblique lines, often crossing one another. The fibers may sometime show slight swellings or knobs, which are considered to be injured inflicted by the mechanical processes to which the fibers have been subjected. Finally, the canal in the center is merely a narrow line in the middle of the fiber.

The third fiber to claim our attention is wool. Again, if possible, obtain some raw wool or, failing that, some threads of woolen material. Proceed as in the case of linen. If you procure the raw wool you will find when you examine some of the fibers in a drop of water that droplets of fatty matter will be seen adhering to them. It is desirable that such fatty matter be removed be-

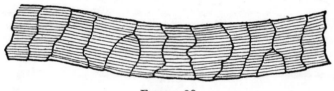

FIGURE 89
Wool

fore proceeding with your examination. To do this, wash a little raw wool gently in water, and pour off the cloudy liquid. Then wash the residual wool with a little alcohol, and then shake it with a little ether or chloroform. Allow the wool to dry and when it is thoroughly dry mount a little in water and examine. Each fiber, you will note, exhibits an outer layer of scales, of which the lower edges are arranged beneath the upper edges of the previous scales like the shingles or tiles on a roof, and an inner core consisting of a number of cells (Figure 89). An interesting fact is that in say an inch of wool from the same kind of sheep there are always the same number or very nearly the same number of scales; and by counting these scales, experts can tell from what animal the wool is derived.

In addition to the cotton, flax, and wool we must add that of silk as a fiber which is extensively woven into a fabric. Silk, as you undoubtedly know, is obtained from the silkworm and is spun by the insect just before it turns into a cocoon. The fiber consists normally of two threads which differ a little in appearance depending on whether the fiber is obtained from

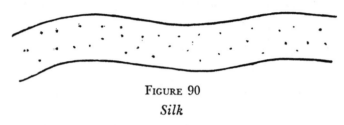

FIGURE 90

Silk

the outer, middle or inner portion of the cocoon. Only the middle layer is used for commerce, as the outer layer is too fine and weak and the inner is so impregnated with a glue, which the silkworm exudes while spinning the threads, as to be useless.

Should you be able to obtain some raw silk, taken from the middle layer of a cocoon, and examine it under the microscope, you will easily see the two parallel fibers of silk and that each fiber is a solid rod, with a smooth lustrous surface and without any sign of lumen or cell structure. It looks for all the world like a tiny thread of solid glass (Figure 90). During the process of manufacture the two constituent threads of each fiber are separated from each other so that if you are unable to obtain the raw silk and must have recourse to the manufactured article, you will not find the two parallel threads. Manufactured silk, however, will look like the raw silk and will appear as almost structureless, nearly cylindrical fibers.

Artificial silk is used to a great extent at present as a substitute for real silk. As a rule it is quite easy to distinguish the artificial product from the real thing, for the imitation usually consists of flat fibers, or at any rate of fibers quite different from the smooth rods of real silk. Should you ever be in doubt, add a little iodine to the fabric under examination. The real silk will be colored brown.

With a knowledge of what the four major fibers look like, you can go ahead on your own initiative and examine other fibers, such as hemp and jute, for example, so that you will be able to recognize them when you meet them.

ADVENTURE 39

We Trace the Life History of Ferns

At certain times of the year you may have observed that the under sides of the leaves of most of our common ferns are covered with small brown or orange spots (sori). If you examine these spots closely or with a hand lens you will find them to consist of a number of small globular objects on stalks, growing in a cluster from the surface of the leaf (Figure 91). These are spore cases (sporangia), and if you scrape off some of them and examine them under the microscope you will find each to consist of a little stalked circular body surrounded by a jointed ring (annulus) (Figure 92). When mature, this ring straightens hygroscopically, breaks the thin side walls, and throws out the numerous small oval cells contained within the circular body. You can see this take place yourself if you will warm the slide, when the ring will straighten itself out and discharge the cells. If, by any chance, nothing should happen, then mount a specimen in water and add a drop of strong glycerine. Then the rupture should take place almost immediately.

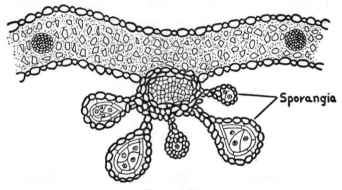

FIGURE 91
Fern Sporangia

The small oval cells which are discharged are spores. These are disseminated by the wind and when they encounter moisture and the other conditions which bring about growth, they germinate. Now when one of these spores germinates, it does not directly produce a fern but instead develops a tiny, green heart-shaped, dainty body, which is capable of making its own food and thus living an independent existence. Such a body, shown in Figure 93, is called a prothallus. As the prothallus grows only in damp, shaded ground you must look for it only in such places. Better still you can raise one yourself by merely scattering the spores of a fern in a glass jar. On the bottom place a bed of moist sand or blotting paper, and cover the jar loosely with a sheet of glass, being sure to keep it moist and warm, and not in too bright a light.

If you examine the prothallus with a hand lens, you will note that from the under surface grow root-like hairs (rhizoids) and that just below the deep cleft of the heart there is a cluster of small, bottle-shaped bodies. These are the archegonia, each of which contains an egg cell. If you cannot make them out very clearly, put a thin section through a part of the prothallus containing one under the microscope. Next look lower down among the rhizoids, near the pointed base, where you will find the antheridia, compact structures in

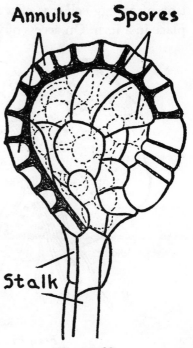

FIGURE 92
Fern Sporangium

which sperm cells are formed. If you remember, you found such structures, that is, an antheridium and archegonium, in the moss plant. (See Adventure 34.) If you also remember, the sperm cells were carried from the antheridium to the archegonium where fertilization of an egg cell was effected. The same thing takes place in a fern. On access of water, the antheridia swell

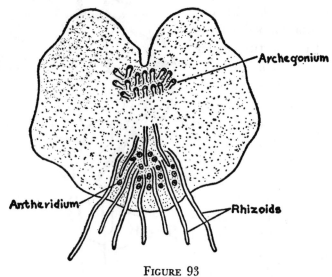

FIGURE 93

Fern Prothallus

and expel the sperm cells, which swim about in the water until one of them enters an archegonium and there fertilizes the egg cell.

As soon as the egg cell is fertilized, it divides into four cells, each of which in turn divides into many cells. One group of cells thus formed gradually develops into a mass, called the foot, which penetrates the prothallus and absorbs nourishment from it. A second group of cells develops into a little root which penetrates the soil, while a third group becomes a small leaf which curls up around the edge of the prothallus until it becomes exposed to air and light, when it begins to manufacture food. Finally the fourth group of cells develops into a stem, which grows slightly downward, and then horizontally beneath the surface of the soil, forming a rhizome. From the stem and rhizome additional leaves and roots develop which at once begin to perform their function of manufacturing food and absorbing the necessary elements for their manufacture, and as the plant begins to grow, the primary leaf and any others which may have developed at the same time, as well as the rhizoids, the foot and prothallus, begin to wither and finally die, leaving in their place the familiar leafy fern plant we know so well (Figure 94).

FIGURE 94
Fern

Geologists tell us that ferns are the oldest form of terrestrial vegetation now in existence and that the coal that is mined today is composed almost entirely of ferns and their allies which lived on the earth some fifty-three million years ago and which constituted the only vegetation of that time. The flowering plants did not appear until nearly thirty million years later.

We are also told that in that far-off age they grew to an enormous size, frequently attaining a height of fifty feet or more. But that is nothing, for in the tropical jungles of today there are ferns that grow from thirty to fifty feet tall with a trunk diameter of several inches. This is quite a contrast to the tiny filmy ferns of the Gulf States and the West Indies that have fronds which measure only an inch or two long.

ADVENTURE 40

We Observe the Circulation of Blood

I remember when I was a boy I was often teased by those older than myself with the warning that if I did not behave in a manner suitable to a young gentleman, my ears and lips would be sewn up by "darning needles." I learned later of course that this was utter nonsense, but the point I wish to make is that with the possible exception of the butterflies no insects strike our imagination so vividly as these darning needles, or dragon flies as they are more properly termed.

Their size and beauty, their swiftness and strength, make them conspicuous to every observing eye. And in their habits and life-history there are the most emphatic contrasts. The nymphs or young live a sordid life in muddy pools; the adults an animated life in the air. Combined with the graceful form and the beautiful colors of the winged insect are fiercely carnivorous tastes. Indeed, we should be inclined to associate such insects with the sweet juices of flowers or some other delicate food, but should we capture one on the wing and examine its mouth, we would find it filled with smaller insects, to be devoured at some later time of leisure.

It is not the adults, however, that we are interested in at the present moment but rather the young, or nymphs as they are called. Examined under the microscope these nymphs show very clearly the tracheal gills and tracheæ—a system of respiration that a number of aquatic insects possess—and the valvular action of the heart, with the consequent flowing of the blood throughout the interior of the animal.

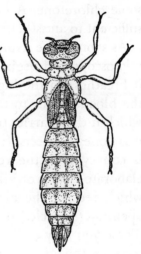

But first of all you must know what one of these nymphs looks like, so you will be able to capture one. They appear as shown in Figure 95 and from this illustration you should have no difficulty in recognizing them. They are not at all nimble and often remain motionless for hours, clinging with their legs to some water

FIGURE 95
Dragon-fly Larva

weed, waiting until some victim comes within easy reach. Even then they do not spring, but merely extend an arm-like appendage secured with spines or teeth with which they grasp their prey. When at rest, this appendage is folded and covers the lower face like a mask. Indeed, it is spoken of as a mask, for when folded it serves to hide its real purpose. Deadly in its action, it is because of its very guise of innocence perhaps the most murderous weapon existing in the whole world of nature. You can observe it through a hand lens and I commend its study to you.

Having obtained one of these nymphs, our next procedure is to examine it under the microscope. It is necessary to use a watch glass rather than a life slide because of its size, and of course we want to study it alive. To keep it quiet, however, we will have to use some chloretone. A one per cent aqueous solution is sufficient to anæsthetize it.

As soon as the nymph becomes quiet, we adjust the microscope and begin our study, first, to find out how it breathes. In the higher animals, as well as in man, the blood is sent to the lungs for a supply of oxygen which it then carries to the tissues. This is not the way it is done in insects, for in these creatures the air itself is conveyed to the remotest tissues by means of an elaborate system of branching air-tubes called tracheæ, which receive the air through a number of outside openings (spiracles) placed along each side of the body. These you may easily see with a hand lens on such insects as the grasshoppers. In a number of aquatic nymphs and larvæ, such as the one we are examining, the spiracles are suppressed and respiration is effected instead by means of gills, which are simply outgrowths of the skin containing tracheæ. In the dragon-fly nymph, such gills, called tracheal gills, are located in

148

the rectum, and if we focus our microscope on this part of the insect's anatomy we shall find it to be furnished with a profusion of delicate tracheal branches. These are bathed by water which is sucked into the rectum and from which the oxygen is derived and then carried through the ramifying tracheæ to all parts of the animal's body.

Having studied these rectal tracheal gills to our satisfaction, we next turn our attention to the circulatory system and observe the action of the heart. Again unlike the higher animals, insects have no system of closed blood-vessels, but the blood wanders freely through the body cavity to enter eventually the heart, which, incidentally, resembles a heart only in being a propulsatory organ. In structure, it consists of a series of chambers on each side of which there is a valvular opening, or ostium, which permits the ingress of blood only, and inside of which there are other valvular folds that permit the blood to flow forward only. It is located well toward the posterior end of the abdomen, just under the skin, and to make it easier for you to identify it, a portion is shown in Figure 96. Extending anteriorly from the heart is a simple attenuated tube,

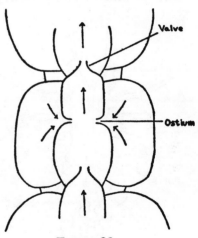

FIGURE 96

Portion of Insect Heart

the aorta, which passes through the thorax and into the head, where it passes under the brain and usually divides into two branches. In the head the blood leaves the aorta and enters the general body cavity.

The blood of an insect consists chiefly of a watery fluid and is usually colorless, although it may sometimes be yellowish from yellow drops of fat, or greenish in herbivorous insects from the presence of chlorophyll.

The course of the circulation may easily be followed in the insect which we are examining, and is as is shown in Figure 97. If we look closely, we shall see currents of blood flowing through the spaces between the muscles, tracheæ and nerves, and bathing all the tissues. We can also distinguish separate outgoing and incoming streams in the antennæ and legs, the returning blood flowing along the sides of the body eventually to enter the ostia of the heart, the chambers of which expand and contract successively from behind forward. At the expansion of a chamber, its ostia open and admit blood; at contraction the ostia

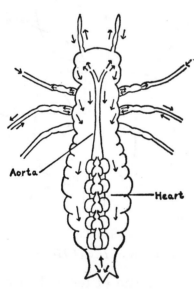

Figure 97

Circulation of Blood in a Nymph

150

close, as well as the valve of the chamber next behind, while the chamber next in front expands, affording the only exit for the blood. The rate at which the heart beats is determined to a great extent by the activity of the insect. The more active it is, the faster the rate of pulsation. And I almost forgot to tell you that the valves operate partly through blood-pressure and partly by muscular action.

ADVENTURE 41

We Do a Bit of Surgery

The keynote of advertisements of dentifrice manufacturers appears to be health and beauty. Now no one can deny the part that good sound teeth play in the health of an individual nor can one deny that healthy, well-formed teeth add to one's appearance. But to be pleasing to the eye, teeth, I think, must have the proper setting. I fail to see any beauty in an individual molar, or in the dentures which sometimes are exhibited in a display case. But I have in mind an instance where the reverse is true. This instance is found in the teeth of an ordinary snail, which, when viewed under the microscope, often are striking and beautiful objects.

These teeth are to be found on strap-shaped ribbons (called lingual ribbons or radulæ) located in the animal's mouth, which, when moved by a powerful muscle, rasp the food material into particles so that they can pass into the esophagus and thence into the stomach.

In order to examine these teeth, it is necessary to remove them from the animal's mouth and to treat them so that they may more easily be seen. Our first step is, of course, to obtain a snail and kill it by placing it in our lethal chamber.* When all signs of life have disappeared, we remove it from the chamber, cut off the head, and soak it in a weak solution of potash until all the soft tissues are destroyed and only the radula remains. We may hasten the process by heating the solution in a test tube, but be careful that it doesn't bump about in the tube and fly out onto the hand, for the potash will remove your skin if allowed to come in contact with it.

When nothing but the radula remains, transfer it to

FIGURE 98
Radula of Snail

water and wash it for some hours to remove all dirt and potash. With a strip of paper on each side to prevent crushing it, it should then be placed between two slides, and the slides bound together by means of string or rubber bands. Holding it in this position, dehydrate and clear it.

On examining the radula under the microscope you will find that it appears somewhat as shown in Figure

* *See Adventure 6.*

98. You will observe that it is armed with sharp, backwardly directed teeth arranged in transverse and longitudinal rows. As these teeth vary in number, form, size and arrangement in different species, they are consequently of great value in classification.

I think most of us know what snails look like, so that a description of them seems somewhat unnecessary. Still a few words might not be out of place. To begin with, a snail's shell, which is the hardened secretion of cells of the fleshy mantle beneath it, is a spiral cone; and twisted and coiled like it is the snail's body, which extends into the apex of the shell. A fresh-water snail has a distinct head, on which are located two tentacles with a small black eye (which is probably not an organ of sight but merely sensitive to light) at the base of each. A land snail has four tentacles.

Snails move about by means of wave-like contractions of muscular fibers of the broad and flat foot. Among the aquatic forms, some breathe by means of gills; others by means of a lung-sac. In some species of snails, the male and female sex organs are in different individuals; in others they are within the same animal. Again, some species lay eggs, depositing them in masses of protecting jelly each of which is in turn enclosed within a capsule of jelly, while others bear their young alive. In cases where eggs are laid, the developing snails may be clearly seen through the jelly. They may be observed turning over and over within their capsules, and as they grow older their eyes and hump may be seen with a hand lens.

We Meet a Champion

In our daily speech, we often use such descriptive phrases, as "graceful as a deer," or "industrious as an ant," or "agile as a monkey," when extolling the virtues of someone we may be discussing. But I can not recall ever having heard of the jumping ability of any individual compared to the jumping prowess of the flea. If my memory serves me right, I remember a statement to the effect that if we could jump in proportion to the jumping ability of the flea, we could jump over the tallest building.

Now as the flea is the greatest jumper known in nature, it represents perfection in one field of endeavor and therefore merits our earnest attention. Perhaps it is not amiss to suggest that we examine one of these creatures and find out what it looks like.

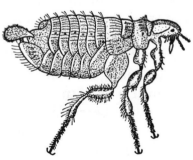

FIGURE 99

Flea

We should experience no trouble in obtaining a flea, for they are abundant enough, as anyone who has a dog will be ready to attest. As a matter of fact, we will make the dog our source of supply, and if we haven't such a pet perhaps your neighbor has one. If so, I am quite sure that he will be more than pleased to cooperate with you.

Upon examining one of these insects, for insects they are, under the microscope you will find it to be a small, wingless creature with sucking mouth-parts, and with a body compressed from side to side to permit it to slip among the hairs of the animal on which it lives (Figure 99). Observe especially the legs, which you will note are particularly modified for leaping.

The eggs are deposited between the hairs, but are not fastened to them, so that when the animal moves about or lies down, they are dislodged and drop to the ground or floor, or wherever the animal may be at the time. Under favorable conditions they will hatch in from two to four days, whereupon the young larvæ, very slender and elongate, and white in color, crawl into the floor cracks or into the rugs and feed on organic matter contained in the accumulated dust and dirt. Within fourteen days after hatching, they spin a delicate silken cocoon from which they emerge four days later as adults.

There are several hundred species of fleas but only a few are troublesome to man. Among these are the human flea, the cat flea, and the dog flea. They annoy man by biting him and they also carry certain disease-producing organisms. Eleven species have been shown to be capable of carrying the bubonic plague, while the dog flea serves as a host for one stage of a species of tapeworm that occasionally infests man.

We Inspect a Spinning Machine

Perhaps you have often wondered as you have seen spiders running deftly along their silken tight-ropes how they ever manage to maintain their hold. Well, if you will amputate a leg and examine the foot under the microscope you will find the answer in the form of comb-like claws with which it is provided (Figure 100).

A great many people seem to have an abject horror

FIGURE 100
Foot of Spider

of spiders and I have often wondered why. To me they are extremely interesting animals, because of their interesting habits, such as home building, mating, care of offspring, prey catching and devices to escape their enemies. In this respect they approach the insects, which many people think they are, but they are no more insects than the lobsters and crabs, although I will admit that all of these various animals have been classified together under one group (Arthropoda) because of certain structural similarities. And if you do not wish to take my word for it, that spiders are not insects, let me point out a few differences. First of all, an insect's body is divided into three parts—the head, thorax and abdomen. Now in spiders, the head and thorax are merged in one piece. Secondly, spiders have no antennæ. The sensory functions which these organs perform in insects is in part performed in spiders by the walking legs. Thirdly, spiders have four pairs of legs to an insect's three. And fourthly, the eyes are simple, as you will see if you examine them. By simple I mean not formed of facets such as we found in the eye of Musca. The eyes, moreover, are usually eight in number and differ in size and arrangement in different sorts of spiders.

There are a great many more differences but these are the most prominent and I think will suffice to show the dissimilarity between these two kinds of animals. There are, however, certain structures unique to spiders which I think might well repay an examination. One of these structures is the first pair of appendages, called cheliceræ (Figure 101).

FIGURE 101

Cheliceræ of Spider

They are situated in front of and above the mouth (which incidentally is but a small opening for the indigestion of juices only, as spiders do not eat solid food) and consist of two segments, a large basal one and a terminal claw-like one. These are the appendages with which the spider seizes and kills its prey, doing so by means of poison secreted by poison glands located in them. The poison passes out through a small

opening near the tip of the claw. The bite of all spiders is therefore poisonous, but there is so little poison and so few spiders are strong enough to bite through the human skin that they are not dangerous. The poison, however, is strong enough to kill insects and to injure larger animals.

A second structure of interest, and one peculiar to spiders, is the book lungs, which are sacs filled with air, each of which opens by a slit-like opening. They may be seen as pale trapezoidal spots with rounded angles on the underside, and near the anterior end of the abdomen (Figure 102). Each book lung contains generally from fifteen to twenty horizontal leaf-like folds, from which the name of book lungs has been derived, and through which the blood circulates. Air entering through the external openings is thus brought into close relationship with the blood. Spiders also possess tracheæ, but they do not ramify to all parts of the body as they do in insects.

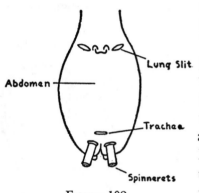

FIGURE 102

Lung Slits of Spider

But perhaps the most interesting of the various structures possessed solely by the spiders is the spinning organs, or spinnerets as they are called, used for spinning threads. They are located at the tail end and on the underside of the abdomen and appear as shown in Figure 103. They are finger-like in form, are usu-

158

ally six in number, and are pierced by hundreds of microscopic tubes, called spinning tubes, through which a fluid (the silk) secreted by a number of silk glands passes to the outside and hardens in the air, forming a thread.

The silk which spiders spin is used for a number of different purposes. Originally it was used for wrapping up their masses of eggs. Later they began to line their nests with it and then to build platforms outside of their retreats and from these developed the snares or webs that are so often held up as marvels of animal ingenuity. The silk that spiders spin makes a better textile than that spun by the silkworm, but the reason it is not used more generally is because of the difficulty of getting enough of it. Compare a strand of spider's silk and a strand of ordinary silk beneath the microscope and see if you can note any differences.

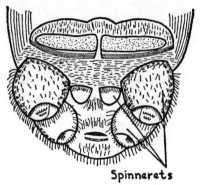

Spinnerets

FIGURE 103

Spinning Organs of Spider

In the webs of the orb-weaving spiders, such as those spun by the Garden-spiders—the large black spiders marked with spots and bands of bright orange and which are so common in late summer—there occurs a peculiar sticky thread which takes the form of a spiral line forming the larger part of the web. This is the trapping portion of the web and if it is touched, ever so lightly, you will find that it will adhere to the object touching it. Moreover, it is very elastic so that when an insect becomes enmeshed in it, its elasticity prevents it from breaking as the insect seeks to escape. If you will

FIGURE 104
Thread of Spider's Silk

examine this sticky and elastic thread under the microscope you will find it to consist of two strands bearing a series of globular drops (Figure 104). The strands are the elastic part of the thread and the drops the sticky portion.

ADVENTURE 44

We Acquire Insight into the Structure of Roots

In preceding adventures we have examined and studied the simplest plants such as the Algæ, Desmids and Diatoms and also some of the higher plants in the evolutionary scale, such as the Mosses, Fungi and Ferns. In the next four adventures we propose to make a study of the highest plants which constitute the familiar land vegetation. These plants include such forms as the trees, shrubs and herbs. Since such forms are so definitely bound up with our very existence, it is well that we should know something of the structure of such organisms, of their chief parts and their functions, and the way in which they operate.

As we all know, a plant—and by plant I now mean the forms we commonly associate with our own well being, such as the geranium we may have in our window, or the maple that stands by the roadside and protects us from the heat of the summer sun, or the radish we raise in our garden for consumption at our table—consists of four main parts. These are the root, the stem, the leaf and the flower which eventually develops into a fruit or seed.

Now I would suggest that we start at the bottom and work our way up; and so we begin with the root, which, though hidden in the soil and therefore perhaps not so well known by most of us as the other parts, is nevertheless a very important organ, for several reasons. In the first place, it anchors the entire plant to the ground and holds the stem in an erect position so that the upper parts of the plant may be maintained in the air and sunlight. In the second place, it absorbs from the soil water and the various mineral salts dissolved in it and which are so essential to the manufacture of food, without which the plant could not continue to exist. And in the third place, the root in some instances, such as the beet, stores large amounts of food, which is just as useful to the plant as it is to ourselves.

Now let us examine a root. Our first step is to obtain a seedling of an oat or radish * or of a grass. Mounting

* A seedling may easily be obtained at any time of the year by merely planting a few seeds in a flower pot or box and watering it daily until the stem begins to push its way out of the ground.

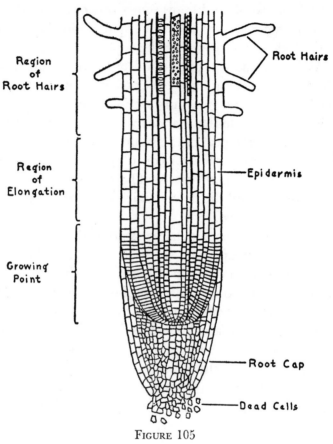

Region
of
Root Hairs

Region
of
Elongation

Growing
Point

Root Hairs

Epidermis

Root Cap

Dead Cells

FIGURE 105

Structure of Root

the root, which should contain a number of hairs, in water on a slide, we place it under the microscope and examine it. We shall find a structure appearing somewhat as shown in Figure 105. Our first glance reveals that it is made up of a great number of small units regularly arranged, which we recognize as cells, differing in size and shape. At the extreme tip, we observe a

162

loose structure which appears to fit over the tip like a thimble. This is the root cap, which is composed of cells which are readily detached, for as the tip of the root is pushed through the soil, the cells of the cap are worn off and continually replaced by new ones. Perhaps you can see some of these loose cells.*

Just above the cap and protected by it you will observe a mass of small more or less rectangular cells and just above this a region of longer cells. The mass of smaller cells is the point where new cells are in the process of formation, while the longer cells are cells that have recently formed and which have since then elongated and by so doing have added to the length of the root. There is a limit to which these cells can elongate and when they have reached this point they are said to have matured; in other words they have acquired the thickened walls and form of mature cells. The remainder of the root is made up of such cells. But these cells are not all alike. They have on the contrary become differentiated and form different parts of the root. What these different parts are we shall see presently.

But first I want to call your attention to the innumerable fine hairs which extend out at right angles from the root just above the region of the elongated cells. On examining these hairs, or root hairs as they are known, you will note that they are finger-like projections from the cells constituting the outside layer or epidermis. Observe what thin walls they have. This is an advantage, for it permits an easy entrance of water

* *If the root cap is not easily distinguishable, obtain a corn or squash seedling in which the cap is more clearly apparent.*

containing in solution the various earth salts which the plant requires in building up its food or carrying on the processes of life.

In order to understand the flow of water into the root and the other activities of this organ, it is essential for us to know something of how a root is made up inside. To obtain such information we must use sections or thin slices cut across the root. These we can cut with a razor blade. Be sure that such sections are very thin, so enough light will pass through them to make the different parts which comprise them distinguishable. A root admirably suited for our purpose is that of a bean or pea seedling. Cut your section through the hairy portion.

On examining your section through the microscope you will find that it looks something like that pictured in Figure 106. The first thing you will notice is that it is composed of cells and that the cells are not all alike. The second thing you will notice is that the cells which have the same general appearance occur together in groups. Now such cells are usually similar not only in structure but also in their activities; and collectively they are called tissues. There are three main divisions of tissues in the hairy portion of the root which we have under examination and each of them in turn is composed of one or more tissues. The three main divisions are the epidermis, cortex, and stele or central cylinder.

The epidermis you should easily recognize as being the outermost layer of cells, from which the root hairs develop. These cells, as you will observe, fit tightly against one another, so that whatever enters a root must pass through and not between them. Within the epidermis is a region of unspecialized cells called parenchyma * which are more or less circular in appearance and which therefore are not entirely in contact with one another, as a result forming spaces which

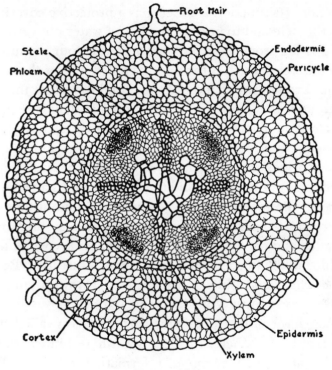

FIGURE 106

Cross Section Through Root

are usually filled with air. This region, comprising the greater part of the root, is known as the cortex, and besides functioning as a passage for water from the epi-

* *Parenchyma cells occur in various other parts of the plant, are of various shapes and sizes, and perform different activities.*

dermis to the stele, sometimes serves as a storage of food in such fleshy roots as the carrot and turnip. Before taking leave of the cortex, you will note that its innermost row of cells is thickened into a sheath or endodermis and forms a conspicuous ring in the cross section. Its function is to serve as a protective covering to the stele and to prevent the loss of water outward.

Passing from the cortex we next turn our attention to the stele, which is the most complex part of the root and through which most of the liquid flows that moves through the plant. The cross or star-shaped figure which you observe in the section is known as the xylem (wood). It is formed of long thick-walled and tough tubes which extend lengthwise in the root and which serve to conduct water and the dissolved substances upward.* Besides the xylem you will also find groups of very small cells. They are also long tubes, but thin walled and collectively they form what is known as the phloem, the function of which is to conduct food. Both the xylem and phloem are enclosed within a ring of cells, located just within the endodermis and form the outer layer of the stele. This ring of cells is called the pericycle. It is here, incidentally, where branch roots originate. They begin as a formation of new cells, which eventually become organized as a root tip. As soon as this root tip is formed, it starts to bore its way out through the cortex into the soil, where it in turn

* *This can be illustrated by a simple experiment. Take a woody tap-root, such as that of a dandelion and let it stand in a colored fluid for about three hours. Remove it and cut a section through it about halfway between the tip and the ground level. Examine with a hand lens and you should be able to distinguish the epidermis, cortex and stele. Which part is colored?*

may give rise to branches, thus forming the root system so familiar to us.

It is only the newest and most delicate parts of the root that produce hairs and are engaged in the active work of absorption, the older parts functioning mainly as carriers. Accordingly the old roots lose much of their characteristic structure and gradually assume more and more the office of the stem until there is no great difference between them. And so, as we follow the plant upwards, we come to the stem which we shall next examine.

ADVENTURE 45

We Examine an Extraordinary Pipe-Line

The stem is that part of the plant we usually think of as the erect, cylindrical, tapering organ which stands above the ground and holds the leaves and flowers extended in the air and light. This is true, of course, but we must not be led into thinking that a stem serves only such a purpose—that of a structural framework for binding the other organs together. On the contrary, it functions also as a water carrier, or pipe-line, for conveying the sap from the roots to the parts where it is needed,* and as a passage for the food manufactured in

* *This can be demonstrated by a simple experiment. If you cut a stem off a plant and place the cut end in colored water you will find that the upper parts of the stem, after a time, will be colored.*

the leaves to the roots, which are living and growing organs and thus require nourishment for continued growth. The stem also serves as a receptacle for food, for inasmuch as it contains chlorophyll, it, like the leaves, also manufactures food. And as this food is frequently an excess supply to that manufactured by the leaves, it sometimes accumulates in the stem, as, for instance, cane sugar in the stem of the sugar cane.

The stem is therefore, as I remarked at the close of the last adventure, apparently much like a root, and if we proceed to examine a cross section of the young stem of the sunflower, for example, we will find that the microscope reveals a structure which is strangely similar to that of a root. Thus we can distinguish the epidermis, which, as in the root, consists of a single layer of cells, the cortex, which as in the root is composed of parenchyma cells, and the stele. We also find that many of the cells composing the stem closely resemble those of the root, but that their arrangement and proportion are different.

The first difference we may notice is that the central part of the stele is not made up of thick-walled xylem cells but of thin-walled parenchyma cells, similar to those we found in the cortex of the root and which collectively are known as the pith. A second difference is that the vascular cylinder is broken up into a circle of distinct patches of vascular tissue lying around the pith and called the vascular bundles. If we bring one of these bundles into the field we will find it to appear as shown in Figure 107. We recognize the xylem as that part toward the center of the stem. It is a rather complex tissue as it contains several kinds of cells that form what is known as tracheæ and tracheids which, shaped like slender tubes, are nothing more than passageways for the rising water. A tracheid is a single elongated cell with pointed ends, while a trachea is formed from a row of short cells and has walls that

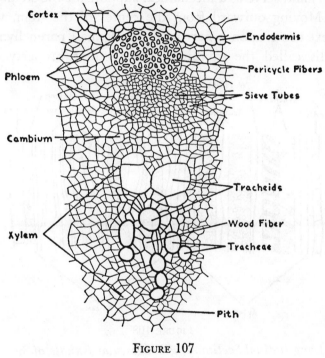

FIGURE 107
Section of Sunflower Stem

are thickened on the inside by rings or spirals. The structure of both a trachea and a tracheid may be seen if we cut and examine a longitudinal section of them. They will appear as shown in Figure 108. As in the root, the cells of the xylem, upon completing their growth, gradually lose their protoplasm, and all vitality ceases. Even the cell sap disappears, and sometimes the walls disintegrate. The dead cells and tissues do not, however, become useless, for they become wood (in the trees forming the heartwood so valuable as timber) and serve as a mechanical support for the stem.

Moving outward from the center of the stem, we next come upon a narrow band of small parenchyma cells called the cambium, the peculiar property of

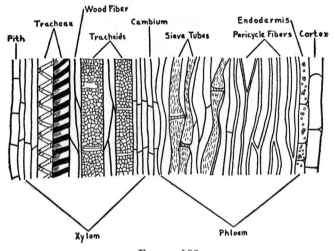

FIGURE 108

Longitudinal Section of Fibrovascular Bundle of Sunflower Stem

which is to form new cells.* Beyond this we find the phloem, which is also like the xylem a complex tissue.

* *I might add as a matter of interest that all the tissues from this point outward are collectively known as the bark; and as the stem grows older the epidermis and frequently also the cortex may disappear and be replaced by cork cells which form the rough hard outer surface of a tree.*

170

It consists essentially of a number of narrow, thin-walled cells known as sieve-tubes,* whose function it is to carry the food made in the leaves down the stem, and a number of smaller elongated cells called companion cells, whose function is not quite understood, but since they are associated with the sieve-tubes it is supposed that they work more or less together as a unit. On the outer side of the phloem is a mass or group of hard fibers which belong to the pericycle, the outer part of the stele, and which frequently may be several layers of cells in thickness.

Most of our common plants have a stem structure such as the sunflower which we have just examined, but there is a larger group of plants which have a stem structure that is quite different. This group includes plants which are of the highest importance to man and includes such forms as the grasses and cereal grains. On examining a cross section of the stem of one of these plants, such as corn for example, we find that the most conspicuous difference is the absence of a visible differentiation into stele and cortex. We observe that the stem is bounded by an epidermis and that scattered throughout it (the stem) there are many vascular bundles. We also observe that these bundles are surrounded by parenchyma cells and that beneath the epidermis are several layers of thick-walled cells forming a supporting tissue, both the cells and the parenchyma cells being not essentially unlike those which we found in the sunflower stem.

Now if we bring one of the vascular bundles into the

* The sieve-tubes are so-called from the sieve-like openings between the connecting walls of the cells which form them.

field we shall find that it is composed of xylem and phloem, as in the sunflower stem, but we shall find certain differences, one of which is the absence of cambium (Figure 109). The phloem, which lies nearest the epidermis, is composed entirely of sieve-tubes and

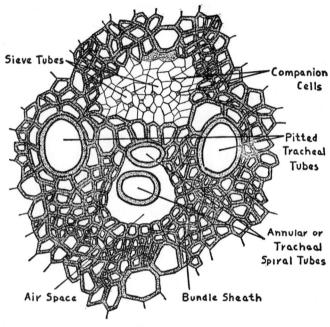

Sieve Tubes

Companion Cells

Pitted Tracheal Tubes

Annular or Tracheal Spiral Tubes

Air Space

Bundle Sheath

FIGURE 109

Cross Section of Vascular Bundle of Corn

companion cells, while the xylem, which lies close to the phloem and toward the center of the stem, is composed of four large openings or ducts. Two of these, called pitted tracheal tubes or ducts because of the bordered pits which cover their outer surface, lie on either side and near the phloem, while the other two, one of which is spiral (from the spiral thickenings of its walls) and the other annular (from the presence of rings on the inside) lie between them. Below these tubes or ducts is a large irregular opening, which is an air space, while between them are smaller cells, parenchyma and small conducting cells. Finally, surrounding the entire vascular bundle are several layers of thick-walled cells which are known as the bundle sheath. Such, then, is the structure of the stem of such plants as the grasses and cereal grains. But before we take our leave of this subject, let me point out one thing, namely the absence of a cambium, and that because of the lack of a cambium the stems of such plants do not increase in diameter by the addition of new cells—in other words, they become no thicker after all their cells have grown to maturity.*

We Tour Through One of Nature's Factories

Of all the different structures that combine to form a plant, the leaves are perhaps the most significant, for it is within them that the food, essential to continued vitality and growth, is manufactured. They are the factories, if you will, where the raw materials of water, absorbed from the soil, and carbon dioxide, absorbed

---

* There are exceptions to every rule; and so there are certain exceptions to the above statement, but such exceptions do not concern us.

from the air, are converted into the finished products sugar and starch. The machines are the chloroplasts * and the motive power for their operation is sunlight. The entire operation or process whereby all this is accomplished is known as photosynthesis, a word which means "building up by means of light."

Now you have probably made many a tour of inspection through various factories either as a part of your education, or through interest in the particular product manufactured. But I daresay that you have never inspected any factory so vitally bound up with your own well-being as the one we are now about to inspect, for do not lose sight of the fact that such a factory is the maintenance of all human existence, not only because it directly supplies us with food but also because it indirectly does so by furnishing food to the animals we slaughter for our own use. The importance of such a factory in the world's economy, I think, is indubitable. For what, indeed, would be the consequences if such a factory ceased to operate? I leave the answer with you.

A leaf, in general, consists of a stalk or petiole and a broad flat thin blade in which can be discerned numerous vascular bundles or veins running in all directions. It is through these veins that the water which enters the plant through the root hairs and moves up the xylem of the root and stem is able to reach every part of the leaf blade, and it is also through these veins that the food which is manufactured in the leaf is removed therefrom and carried down the stem and then distributed throughout the plant.

Like that of the root and stem, the structure of the

---

* Chloroplasts are bodies containing chlorophyll.

leaf is differentiated into groups of cells. First of all is the outermost layer or epidermis, from which grow any hairs with which the leaf may be covered. If we peel off some of the epidermis of the leaf of a geranium for example, preferably from the under side, and examine it under the high power of the microscope, we will find it to be composed of more or less irregular spaces, with

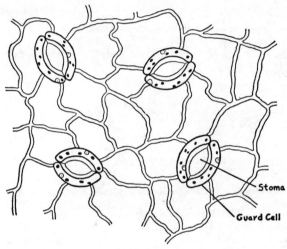

FIGURE 110
Under Epidermis of a Geranium Leaf

the outlines fitting into each other like the tiling of a floor or the blocks of a Chinese puzzle (Figure 110). We recognize the spaces as cells and the lines as the cell walls. Between some of these cells we will find pairs of kidney-shaped or crescent-shaped bodies, so placed, with the ends of the crescents touching, to form a small elliptical opening between them. The opening is a stoma (from the Greek word meaning mouth) and its function is to permit air to enter into the tissues of the leaf as well as to provide a means of escape in the form of vapor for any excess of water which the plant absorbed from the soil and which it could not use in the manufacture of food. The kidney-shaped bodies are known as guard cells and are so called because they open or close the stoma. They operate hygroscopically,

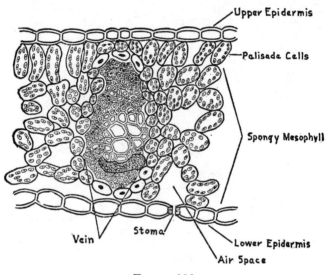

FIGURE 111
Cross Section of Leaf

expanding, and by so doing open the stoma, when they become turgid or filled with an abundance of water. Conversely, by collapsing they close the stoma. Then they lose their turgidity through a lack or dearth of water.

Having examined the epidermis to our satisfaction, we next turn to a study of the internal anatomy of a leaf. For this purpose we need a cross section. To obtain such a section we roll a leaf blade and then with a razor we cut the thinnest slice possible through the roll. We then take a small bit of this section—which should be so thin as to appear almost transparent—mount it in a drop of water on a slide and examine with the high power of the microscope (Figure 111).

The first thing to observe is the horizontally flattened cells of the upper and lower epidermis. Between these two layers of cells you will next find cells containing numerous chloroplasts. These cells are collectively known as the mesophyll of the leaf, and it is here that food manufacture takes place. Some of them—those just beneath the epidermis—are vertically elongated cells which stand rather closely together and which are known as palisade cells from their fancied resemblance to the palisades with which forts were surrounded in early times. Below this layer the cells are collectively known as the spongy mesophyll because of the large air spaces by which they are separated. These air spaces are connected with one another and with the stomata * and ramify throughout the leaf. Finally, and also located in the mesophyll, are the veins, which are vascular bundles connected with the stem which consist, as in the root and stem, of xylem and phloem. Such then is the structure of a typical leaf blade, consisting in summary of a mesophyll composed of veins and cells containing chloroplasts and covered with an epidermis pierced by small holes. This is the factory we set out to inspect; and now that we know the machines of which such a factory consists, let us see how they

* *Plural of stoma.*

operate in turning out the products for which they were assembled.

First of all, air containing carbon dioxide enters through the stomata and passes into the air spaces. Upon reaching the cell walls of the mesophyll, the carbon dioxide dissolves in the water and in solution (as carbonic acid) diffuses to the chloroplasts, where, under the influence of light and chlorophyll the carbon dioxide and water combine to form sugar and oxygen. The sugar thus formed may either be converted into starch in the chloroplast or into some other substance, such as oil, fat * or cellulose, or may be used to supply energy, while the oxygen diffuses as dissolved oxygen to the cell wall and passes off into the air spaces as gaseous oxygen, and finally out through the stomata into the air. Meanwhile, as this process goes on, the substances manufactured, be they sugar, starch or fat,

* Should you not believe me when I say that such substances are manufactured in the leaf, you can find out for yourself very easily. If you have studied chemistry you may recall that iodine is an indicator of starch, which it colors blue. To find out if there is any starch in leaves, crush a few leaves of bean or sunflower, for instance, and soak in alcohol until all the chlorophyll is dissolved out. Then rinse them in water, and soak the leaves thus treated in an iodine solution (four to one dilution of the tincture in water) for a few minutes. Remove and wash them and hold them up to the light. You should find a number of blue spots, indicating the presence of starch.

If you also recall, Fehling's solution, which can be obtained in a drug store, is used in testing for grape sugar, which is the kind manufactured in leaves. To find out if there is any such sugar in leaves, express the sap from fresh specimens. Now heat a teaspoonful of Fehling's solution in a test tube until it comes to the boiling point and then pour in a few drops of the sap. Heat again. A red precipitate should form, indicating the presence of sugar.

To test for fat, place some macerated alcanna root in a vessel with alcohol enough to cover it. Leave for an hour, then add an equal amount of water and filter. Next immerse a few leaves, which should be dried. The presence of fat will be indicated by the appearance of deep red spots.

are carried through the veins and into the stem, whence they are distributed to the various parts of the plant.

ADVENTURE 47

We Learn That Flowers Are Not Merely Ornamental

We now come to the flower which is unquestionably the most striking part of the plant. Indeed, so prominent and distinctive is this part of the plant that to many people the study of Botany implies the study of flowers. Of course, something can be said for this belief because the beautiful colors, the attractive fragrance, and the striking forms to which they owe their esthetic charm have appealed to mankind since time immemorial.

Now flowers were not designed to delight the senses of man but to perpetuate the species to which they belong. In other words, they are reproductive structures. But strangely enough they cannot fulfill their destiny without outside aid; and this outside aid takes the form of wind and animals, especially insects. Wind as an agent leaves much to be desired, primarily because it cannot be depended upon. The flowers learned this to their dismay ages ago. Insects, however, were a different matter, for they could be depended upon provided they were offered some sort of inducement, for surely in a world of selfishness they could not be expected to work for nothing. So in return for their active help, the flowers decided to offer them nectar.

In this age of commercial rivalry, what does a business man do to sell his product? He advertises. And the better advertising he can put out the greater his sales will be. Flowers learned this ages ago. And so they assumed colors pleasing to the eye and odors delightful

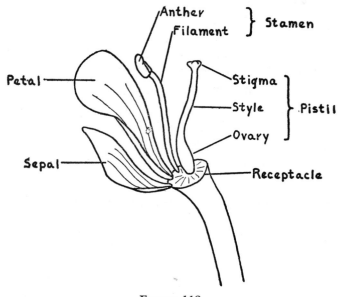

FIGURE 112
Diagram of Simple Flower

to the sense of smell. And the insects reciprocated accordingly. The next time you sniff the delightful fragrance of some gorgeous bloom, do not be misled into believing that such charms were created for your especial benefit.

180

In spite of their striking external multiformity, flowers are comparatively simple and uniform in their mode of construction. In Figure 112 we have drawn a diagram of a typical simple flower, to which you can compare almost any blossom you may have at hand. First we have the receptacle which is the tip of the floral stem. Then we have the outer greenish leaves called sepals, which collectively are known as the calyx. Next we have the brightly colored leaves or petals

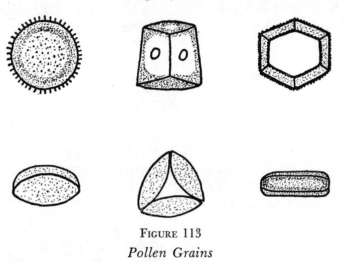

FIGURE 113
Pollen Grains

which collectively are known as the corolla. Within this corolla we have a whorl of appendages, the stamens, each of which consists of a slender cylindrical stalk, the filament, bearing at its tip an enlarged rounded yellow body, the anther. If you examine the anther with a hand lens, you will see that it opens by longitudinal slits which permit the escape of a yellow powder. This powder, called pollen, will be seen under the lens to consist of little yellow grains, within which develop the male or sperm cells. These grains are of different shapes, colors, and sizes in different plants. And if you will examine such grains from different plants you will find them extremely beautiful objects (Figure 113), sometimes having surfaces that are beautifully grooved and striated.

Within the whorl of stamens, and occupying the center of the flower, is the pistil, made up of modified leaves called carpels. It is seen to consist of a hollow rounded base, the ovary, tapering upward to a short

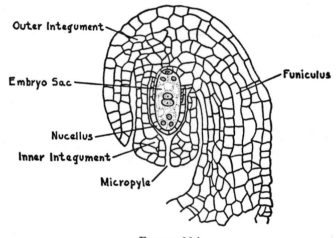

FIGURE 114
Section of Lily Ovule

cylindrical stalk called the style and ending in a roughened area known as the stigma.

Now if you select a flower that has begun to wither, so that the ovary is well developed, and open the ovary, you will find that it contains a number of small roundish whitish bodies, within each of which, in a special sac, lies a female sex cell—the egg cell. These bodies are called ovules and later they will develop into seeds.

In Figure 114 the structure of a typical ovule is shown. The innermost part is the relatively large egg sac, in which lie several small cells, the most important of which is the egg cell, usually the largest of them, and which when fertilized grows gradually to an embryo plant within the sac. The sac is embedded within a rounded mass of tissue, the nucellus, and this in turn is inclosed by one or two integuments, which grow up to surround the nucellus from a stalk, the funiculus, leaving, however, a small opening, the micropyle.

Such in brief is the structure of a typical flower. Now we shall see how such a flower operates. The first step is the transfer of the pollen to the pistil. It so happens that, in general, the pollen must be transferred to the pistil of another flower to effect fertilization of the egg cell and this is achieved by wind or, more usually, by insects. When a pollen grain falls on the surface of the stigma it begins to germinate by sending a slender, delicate, thin-walled tube down into the substance of the pistil. This tube, carrying near its top the sperm cells, gradually grows down through the tissues of the style. If you cut the thinnest possible section through a freshly pollinated pistil of a lily or other large flower * and examine under the microscope, you can watch the pollen tubes as they descend through the style toward

* Better still obtain, if possible, a pollinated strand of corn silk. This is only a very much elongated style and is excellent for our purpose as it is so thin and transparent that no section need be made, and the tube can be traced as it works its way down through the entire length of the thread-like style to the ovary.

the ovary (Figure 115). As a rule, the time required for the tube to penetrate to the ovary is a matter of only a few hours, but in some plants, as in the crocus, it takes from one to three days, and in the orchids, from ten to thirty days. In some flowers the pistil is hollow, affording a free passage to the pollen tube; in others it is solid

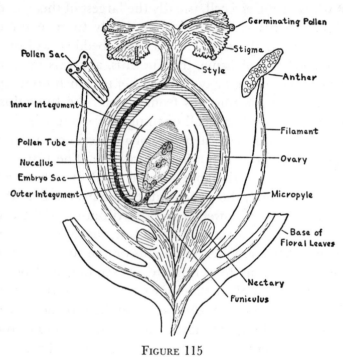

FIGURE 115

Diagrammatic Section of Simple Flower

and in such instances the pollen tube eats its way down, as it were.

On reaching the ovary, the pollen tube at once approaches an ovule, which it enters through the micropyle, and eventually reaches the embryo sac, which

184

every ovule contains and within which, near the micro-pyle, lies the egg cell. Here it discharges the sperm cells, which at once enter the egg cell, effecting what is known as fertilization. Upon the fertilization of the egg cell, a series of cell divisions take place, resulting in a mass of cells which develops into an embryo plant. Meanwhile the ovule has been stimulated into growth and gradually develops into the seed, while the ovary in its turn grows into a fruit. At the same time, the sepals, petals, stamens, style and stigma, their function accomplished, wither and fall away.

ADVENTURE 48

We Investigate the Structure of Paper

When man first began to write, he probably used such natural objects as stones, leaves, or bits of wood on which to inscribe his thoughts; and it was not until the celebrated papyrus was invented in Egypt, many hundred years before the Christian era, that a real paper was used for this purpose. The modern process of making paper, as a thin layer of cellulose derived from fibrous vegetable material reduced to a pulp in water, was discovered by the Chinese and introduced into Europe by the Arabs in the eleventh century. Cotton was the first material used and flax as early as 1100 A.D. while the use of wood pulp appears to have been first suggested by the French naturalist, Reaumur, in

1719. He derived his idea from a study of the way in which wasps construct their nests from this material.

At the present time such substances as linen and cotton rags, hemp and wood pulp are used in the manufacture of paper. The raw stock is first treated with some strong chemical in order to break it up, to dissolve the cementing gums, and to separate the cellulose—which is always the principal constituent of paper—in as pure a form as possible. The crude material is then boiled with a strong alkali and washed in a tank from which the waste water is removed by a revolving drum. The paper stock is next bleached and then passed through various other processes until finally the fully prepared pulp passes to the paper machines, where it is spread

FIGURE 116
Tracheid of Conifer

in a thin sheet over a moving endless belt of wire cloth, from which the fibrous material, deposited in a fine and even layer, is carried on through felted rollers which press out the last of the water and compact its texture.

There are a good many different kinds of paper manufactured today as well as cardboards which are really a kind of paper. The finest and whitest paper is made from linen rags and the strongest from unused linen and hemp, while the so-called Manila paper is made from jute. Papers made from the various raw products have certain well-defined qualities according to the nature of the substance from which it was made, and accordingly it is often desirable to learn the composition of a certain paper to see if it fulfills the specifications which it should meet. Here the microscope is brought into use. From the drastic treatment to which

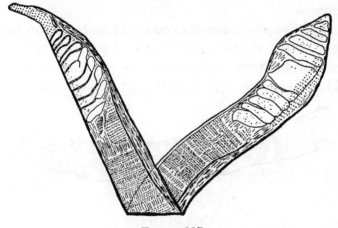

FIGURE 117
Tracheid of Birch

the raw products have been subjected, such fibers as survive are necessarily but mere fragments, yet they are often large enough to be made out. For instance, if we examine a piece of linen rag paper we should expect to find some flax fibers. They will probably be badly battered and torn yet recognizable. If we also examine a piece of cotton rag paper we should find the characteristic cotton fibers, that we examined in Adventure 38. And if you followed my suggestion of examining a fiber of jute you should find such fibers in a piece of Manila paper, such as is used for envelopes, wrappers and other similar articles.

To examine a piece of paper with the microscope, it should be torn into small bits and boiled in a one per cent solution of caustic soda. The wet pulp is then washed on a fine sieve and broken up by shaking in water. A small piece is then placed on a slide and examined.

If, in the piece of paper you are examining, you find none of the characteristic fibers with which you are familiar, but fibers like those shown in Figures 116 and 117, then you know that the paper has been made from

FIGURE 118
Cells of Straw

wood pulp, in the first instance from a conifer, such as spruce, fir, pine or hemlock, and in the second instance from a tree such as the poplar or birch. Finally, if you find fibers that appear like that shown in Figure 118, then you have a paper that was manufactured from the stems of grasses or grains. For a fuller explanation of the structure of such fibers see Adventure 38. In your examination of paper do not conclude from the examination of a single piece that the paper is entirely made up of the fiber which you found, for frequently paper is made up of several different fibers so it is well to examine a number of pieces before you pronounce your judgment as to the composition of the paper you are examining.

We Train Our Lens on Two Familiar Creatures

I think most of us are familiar with the little animals popularly known as the "thousand legs" which are to be found in dark, moist places where they feed principally on vegetable substances (Figure 119). The body is nearly cylindrical and consists of from about twenty-five to more than one hundred segments, depending upon the species. Each of these segments contain a pair of scent glands, which open laterally, and most of them

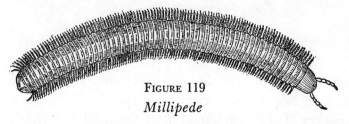

FIGURE 119
Millipede

in addition bear two pairs of leg-like appendages. On the head are the mouth parts, the eyes, and a pair of antennæ, which, if examined under the microscope, will be seen to be covered with hairs that are olfactory in function.

In spite of their numerous legs, the Millipedes, as these animals are properly called, move very slowly. The eggs are laid in damp earth and on hatching produce young which have few segments and only three pairs of legs, looking strangely similar to the wingless insects such as we studied in Adventure 37.

If we are at all acquainted with these animals then, I am sure, we are also familiar with the "hundred legs" or Centipedes (Figure 120), as they are often found in association with the Millipedes in such places as under stones and under the bark of logs. The body is flat

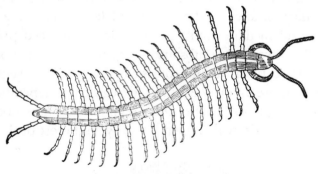

FIGURE 120
Centipede

and consists of from fifteen to over one hundred and fifty segments, also according to species. With the exception of the one just back of the head and the last two, each of the segments bears one pair of legs, which, unlike those of the Millipedes, carry the animals rapidly over the ground.

The most interesting feature of the Centipedes is the pair of poison claws which are attached to the segment just back of the head and which should be examined under the microscope. Their terminal joints, which are very sharp, contain the ducts of the poison glands, from which a poison is secreted that is used in killing insects, worms and other small animals for food. Their poison has no effect on us, beyond perhaps leaving a red spot on the skin, but there are some Centipedes in the tropical countries that reach a foot in length and whose bite is not only painful but dangerous.

ADVENTURE 50

We Behold an Animal That Swims on Its Back

If you should examine a spring pool, such as is formed in early spring by the melting snow, you may observe the presence of a number of small animals that appear to be swimming about on their backs. On closer scrutiny you will find them to be pale reddish in color, with a stout and rather large body and numerous broad hairy or bristly flattened feet or legs that are somewhat leaf-like in appearance (Figure 121).

These animals belong to a group known as the Phyllopoda which is from the Greek and means leaf-footed. Evidently whoever named the animals originally thought that the legs were the most characteristic feature of these animals, and when you examine them under the microscope I think you will agree with him. There are a number of species of Phyllopods, but the one that we are about to examine is called the Fairy Shrimp. Why, I don't know.

The feet, which are arranged in eleven pairs, are used for swimming. At a point near where they are attached to the body you will find a flattened plate. This is used in breathing. The head, on which are located two black eyes, elevated on the ends of short stalks, is rather large, and in the male the

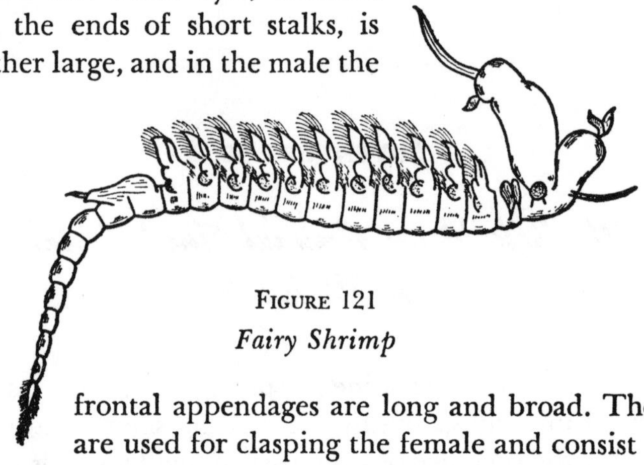

FIGURE 121
Fairy Shrimp

frontal appendages are long and broad. They are used for clasping the female and consist of an upper half, which is broad and thick, and a stiff, bristle-like prolongation, with a short bristle-like tooth on the inner side at the point where the two parts are connected.

The Fairy Shrimp is not confined to spring pools but may be found in almost any body of fresh water. The reason I mentioned spring pools is to bring out an interesting feature of this animal. Such pools, as you well know, gradually dry up as spring advances until they eventually disappear altogether. And so of course do the Fairy Shrimps; I mean they also disappear. But in the following spring, when the pools reappear, or, more accurately, are reformed, the Fairy Shrimps will also be found to reappear. Perhaps you have already observed this phenomenon. Now the question is, what happened to the animals meanwhile? Before I answer I must point out that the animals seen in one spring are not the same individuals that were seen the year before, which would seem to make the whole thing more perplexing than ever. But the answer is a very simple one and is to be found in the eggs, of which there are two sets or kinds—summer eggs and winter eggs.

The summer eggs, which are thin-shelled, are carried by the mother in a brood pouch and hatch without fertilization; in other words they are designed so as to bring about a rapid increase of the species during the wet season. The winter eggs, which are laid later, do not hatch immediately but fall to the bottom, where they require a long time for development. They are thick-walled and may be dried or frozen without injury. In other words, they are designed to preserve the species through times of drought and cold. Accordingly, as the pools dry up, the animals eventually die off, but the life cycle is carried on by the winter eggs which remain, to hatch ultimately when the pools are reformed in the following spring.

We Receive a Lesson in Evolution

To my mind one of the most impressive features of Nature is the manner in which the body structure of animals has become adapted to their environment and how various organs have become modified for specific uses. Insects exemplify both of these points more than any other group of animals.

Consider, for instance, the water beetle known as Hydrophilus (Figure 122) which can be found in almost any body of fresh water. Doesn't its general form remind one of a boat, and don't its long legs resemble oars? Exactly! Here, then, is a case in point to illustrate how the body structure of this animal has become adapted to an aquatic existence, for the smoothly elliptical contour and the polished surface serve to lessen resistance. Here also is an illustration of how an organ has become modified for specific use, for, as you will note if you examine one of them under the microscope, the legs are covered with hairs which aid them in propelling the insect through the water. When swimming,

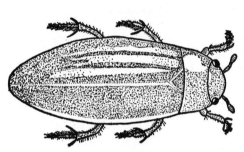

FIGURE 122

Hydrophilus

the "stroke" is made by the flat surface, aided by these hairs; but on the "recover," the leg is turned so as to cut the water, while the hairs fall back against the tarsus from the resistance of the water, as the leg is being drawn forward.

The legs of insects have become modified for a great many purposes. We have already seen two examples of this—in the adhesive pad of the house fly (Adventure 7) and the pollen basket of the Honey Bee (Adventure 13). Speaking of the Honey Bee, if you will examine one of the bee's front legs, you will find a little round notch on the inside of the large joint that is nearest the bee's foot and observe that over it a little spike or pointed brush of stiff hairs projects down from the part of the leg above the joint (Figure 123). This is the

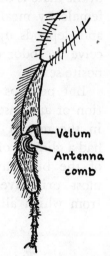

Velum

Antenna comb

FIGURE 123
Antenna Comb of Honey Bee

bee's comb and is used for cleaning the antennæ. Ants also have a device for cleaning the antennæ, but it differs from the groove and brush of the bee and consists instead of two little combs (Figure 124).

The antennæ, too, have become modified for special uses. We have already seen that the antennæ of the male mosquito (Adventure 20) are highly developed organs of hearing. If you will compare the antennæ of the male and female of the cecropia moth you will find that the antennæ of the male are larger and more feathered than those of the female (Figure

125) and also have more segments. In this insect the antennæ are olfactory and the reason for their greater development in the male is that the male seeks out the female by means of the sense of smell and depends upon his antennæ to perceive the odor emanating from the opposite sex.

But perhaps the greatest differentiation of any insect organ is to be found in the mouth parts. We have already had a glimpse of this in the sucking tube of the butterfly (Adventure 24). The most primitive type of mouth parts, from which all others have developed, is the biting or man-dibulate type. The various parts that compose such a type can easily be made out in the common grasshopper. If we obtain one of these insects and examine its head we will find it to look as shown in Figure 126. At the lower end is a plate that looks like an upper lip. That is what it is, and it is called the labrum. Should we insert the point of a pin under it, we will find it to be quite

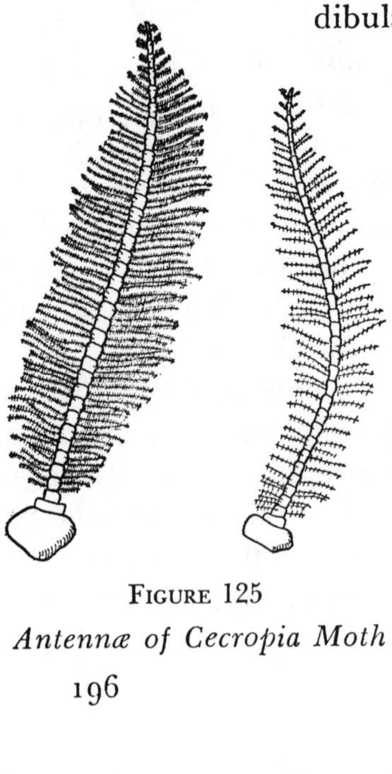

FIGURE 124
Ant's Comb

FIGURE 125
Antennæ of Cecropia Moth

196

stiff and horny and movable up and down upon the hinge that joints it to the face. The labrum covers the mandibles in front and pulls back food to these organs. The mandibles or jaws proper are single-jointed and are broad, short, solid, with a toothed cutting and grinding edge, adapted for biting. Unlike our jaws which move up and down, they move sideways. Behind the mandibles are the lower jaws, or maxillæ. You will find them to be divided into three lobes, the inner one armed with teeth or spines, the middle un-armed and spatula-shaped, while the outer forms a five-jointed feeler called the maxillary palpus. These maxillæ are accessory jaws, and serve to hold and arrange the food to be ground by the true jaws. Next comes the

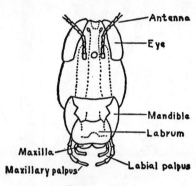

FIGURE 126

Head of Grasshopper

lower lip, or labium, which forms the floor of the mouth and helps in carrying food to the mandibles and maxillæ. Within the mouth, and situated upon the labium, is the tongue, called the hypopharynx, which is a medium fleshy organ.

Such are the mouth parts of a typical biting insect. Now all insects do not bite; a great many, such as the butterflies and mosquitoes, suck, and accordingly their mouth parts must be of different construction. They have been developed, however, from the biting mouth parts and so we should expect to find the same parts but perhaps formed somewhat differently.

Let us obtain a butterfly such as we examined in Adventure 24 and again look at its mouth parts, which as you will recall consisted essentially of a long spring-

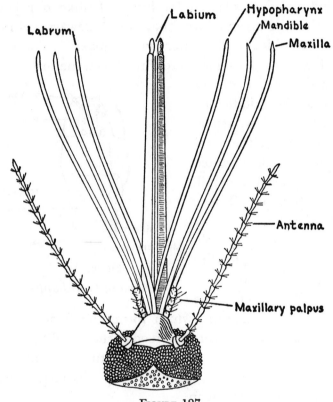

FIGURE 127

Mouth Parts of Female Mosquito

like tube by means of which it sucks up nectar (Figure 54). Looking at the mouth parts closely you will find that the mandibles are rudimentary while, on the other

198

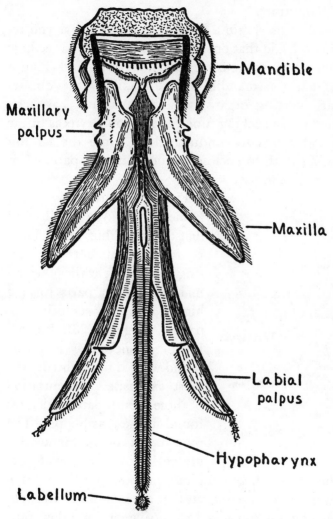

Mandible

Maxillary
palpus

Maxilla

Labial
palpus

Hypopharynx

Labellum

FIGURE 128
Mouth Parts of Honey Bee

199

hand, the maxillæ have been enormously lengthened, grooved on the inner sides and fitted together to form the "soda straw."

Next let us obtain a female mosquito, for as you remember, I said that only the female sucks, and see how her mouth parts are constructed. Here we find (Figure 127) that the mandibles and maxillæ are delicate, linear, piercing organs, while the labrum has been formed into a sucking tube. The hypopharynx is linear also and serves to conduct saliva, while the labium forms a sheath to enclose the other mouth parts when they are not in use.

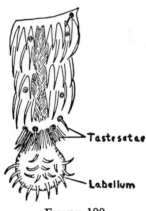

FIGURE 129

Taste Organs of Honey Bee

Finally let us turn to the Honey Bee. We shall find that the mandibles are well-developed instruments for cutting purposes, while the remaining mouth parts form a highly complex suctorial apparatus (Figure 128). Indeed, in the Honey Bee is to be found what is undoubtedly the most exquisite differentiation of those mouth parts which we found in the grasshopper. The mouth parts of the Honey Bee are really too complex to describe in detail, but for our purpose it will be sufficient, I think, to point out that the mandibles are well-developed instruments for cutting or for other purposes such as shaping the wax used in building cells, while the maxillæ have been greatly lengthened and

200

hollowed out on the undersides (Figure 128). The lower lip and also its two labial palpi have also been lengthened, and so when all these five parts are closely held together, they form a tube through which nectar is sucked by the expansion and contraction of the tube itself. The tongue terminates in a spoon or labellum on which may be seen short setæ (Figure 129). These are organs of taste. The wasp, known as the Yellow Jacket, also has similar organs. They are located on the maxillæ and may be seen as pits, each

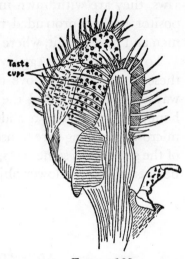

FIGURE 130

Taste Organs of Yellow Jacket Wasp

with a cone, or peg, projecting from its base (Figure 130).

In the female of some insects the end of the abdomen is prolonged into an egg-laying instrument called an ovipositor. An exceptionally good ovipositor is to be found in the insects known as Sawflies, so named because the ovipositor is shaped like a saw and is used for boring a hole into wood or other similar substance where the eggs are to be laid. Here the ovipositor consists of a pair of toothed saws which slide along a firm piece that supports each blade. These saws are worked alternately (one being protruded while the other is drawn back) with great rapidity, and when not in use lie in a fissure beneath a sort of arch formed by the last segment of the body. When a slit has been made by the saws, they are withdrawn into the sheath and the ovipositor is then protruded from the end of the abdomen and into the slit, where an egg is deposited.

To examine this egg-laying device obtain one of these insects, and remove the ovipositor in the same way that you extracted the stinging apparatus of the honey bee. Place on a slide and examine under the microscope, being sure to use a high power, as the teeth of the saw are, in some cases, so fine that they are apt to be overlooked if a lower objective is used.

ADVENTURE 52

We Perform a Major Operation

In this adventure we are going to perform a major operation, and our "patient," or should I say victim, is going to be one of those large beetles which are usually found, under cover, in gardens, fields and open woods. Their common name is Caterpillar Hunters and their name is well given, for they feed for the most part on the larvæ of butterflies and moths. Indeed, one of them at one time was brought over from Europe to aid in fighting the Brown-tail Moth.

Most of them are black but some of them are beautifully colored. Try to obtain one of these because we are going to examine one of the wing covers under the microscope. First, of course, we must kill it in our lethal chamber, and when all signs of life have disappeared we sever one of the wing covers, which are called elytra, from the body, and on viewing it through the microscope we will find that it is covered with numerous striations or pits. Now the colors of insects are classified according as they are pigmental due to internal pigments—or structural due to structures that cause interference or reflection of light. For the most part, the colors of insects are due to internal pigments, but in many instances they are due to structures. Thus, for instance, the brilliant iridescent hues of many butterfly scales are due to the diffraction of light by fine, closely parallel striæ, the particular color produced depending upon the distance between the striæ.

In beetles, such as the one we are examining, the brilliant blues and greens, and iridescence in general, are produced by the minute lines or pits that we found on the wing cover, which act as revolving prisms to disperse different wave-lengths of light in different directions, the combined result being iridescence.

Leaving the wing cover, we next proceed to the object for which we originally obtained the insect, and that is the examination of its alimentary or digestive tract. First of all we must soak the insect in water for a day or two in order to soften it up for the operation. Then, grasping its body, we pull very gently upon the head with a pair of forceps. We should be able to remove not only the head, but also the esophagus, the stomach and the other parts that go to form the digestive system. If this method is not successful, however, we may remove it by cutting away the dorsal wall of

the body and then dissecting it from the body cavity.*
When ready for examination it should appear as
shown in Figure
131. First we have
the esophagus,
which is a simple
tube of small and
uniform caliber,
whose function is
to conduct food.
The esophagus in
turn is succeed-
ed by the crop,
which is conspic-
uous as a simple
dilatation. Here
the food is acted
upon by a secre-
tion which con-
verts albuminoids
into assimilable
peptone-like sub-
stances. Follow-
ing the crop is an
enlargement known as the proventriculus, or gizzard,
which is lined with teeth for straining the food.

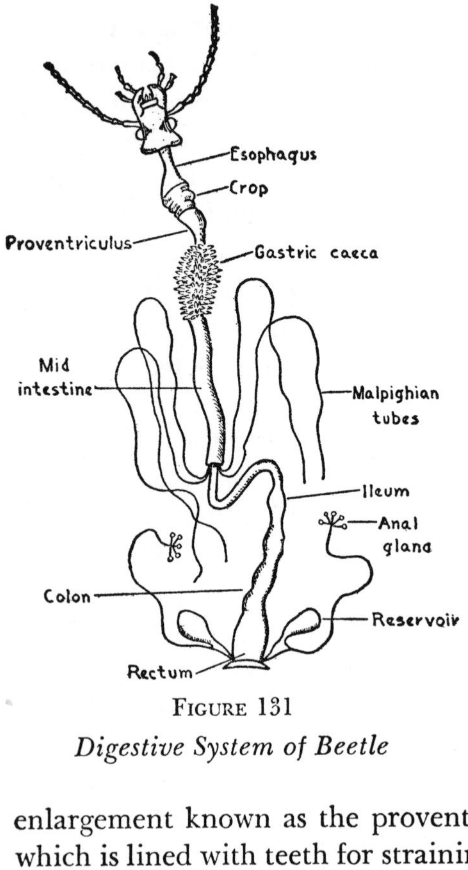

FIGURE 131

Digestive System of Beetle

The proventriculus in turn opens into the mid-intestine or stomach, which is a simple tube of larger
caliber than the esophagus. The chief function of the
stomach is absorption. Into the anterior portion of the

---

* *The entire alimentary canal should then be washed with water and
stained in borax-carmine.*

stomach enter a number of glandular tubes, or gastric caeca, which secrete a fluid that probably aids in digestion.

After the stomach comes the hind intestine, which is made up of three regions—the ileum, colon and rectum. The ileum is rather long and slender and its function is absorption; it is here that absorption of the fluid portion of the food takes place. The colon contains indigestible matter and the waste products of digestion; and it in turn expands into the rectum, which terminates in the anus. The rectum is thick-walled and strongly muscular, and its office is to expel excrementitious matter, consisting largely of indigestible substances. Opening into the intestine immediately behind the stomach you will find a number of long, slender tubes. These tubes, known as the Malpighian tubes, in function are analogous to our kidneys, relieving the body of the waste products and containing a great variety of substances, chief among which are uric acid and its derivatives.

ADVENTURE 53

We Prove That Appearances Are Sometimes Deceptive

A group of plants of peculiar fascination because of the extreme beauty of their microscopic structure and the interest of their life cycles, is that known as the Slime Molds. These are the slimy, filmy mold-like masses sometimes considerable in size and quite visible to the naked eye, which may be found in damp, shaded places where they creep over rotting wood, decaying leaves, and other similar substances.

The ordinary plant body, known as a plasmodium, is nothing but a mass of protoplasm, in consistency much like the white of an egg and lacking walls but containing many nuclei. It is typically white or yellowish in color but may also be pink, violet or other tints, and in some species may be compact in form and a few millimeters in diameter, while in others it may be a loose open network or an irregular film or sheet several inches across. As it never displays the green of chlorophyll, it is unable therefore to manufacture its own food, which it obtains instead from the damp organic substratum upon which it lives, ingesting, like the Amœba, solid pieces of substance from which it later digests the nutritive materials.

In the vegetative state the plasmodium is motile, moving over the substratum much after the manner of the Amœba. This may not be apparent at first, but should we chance upon a patch of plasmodium and keep it under observation for a few hours we shall find that it does not remain in the same spot but frequently moves considerable distances and within a comparatively short space of time. Ordinarily the plasmodium is sensitive to light, and while in the vegetative state stays fairly close to moist and shady places, but when about to produce spores it emerges from the shade into drier, more elevated and more highly lighted places, where it proceeds to develop spore-containing structures (sporangia).

While searching for one of these Slime Molds we may find, in very old logs that have reached an extreme of decay, a very fine and velvety powder, deep reddish-brown in color. If we take home some of this powder and examine it under the microscope we shall find it to be composed of numberless structures that appear something like that shown in Figure 132. These are the spore-containing structures or sporangia mentioned above and they will be seen to consist of a supporting stalk and an enlarged upper portion, containing, within a hardened envelope, a lacy-delicate framework called the capillitium in which are enmeshed cellulose-walled spores (Figure 132). In some species, the sporangia are quite elaborate and beautifully colored and are delightful objects to view through the microscope.

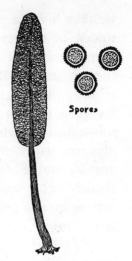

Spores

FIGURE 132

Capillitium and Spores of Slime Mold

When the spores, which are borne on the capillitium, become matured, they are released by the breaking of the envelope and the swelling and hygroscopic movements of the capillitium, and disseminated by the wind. On reaching a moist place they at once begin to germinate and form one-celled free-swimming organisms called zoospores that recall to our mind Euglena. We can see these zoospores for ourselves if we take home a plasmodium that we may find in the woods, or wherever we may go in search of one, and examine some of it (the smallest smear will do) under the microscope. Be sure, however, to keep it moist at all times. In order to do so while transporting it home I suggest that you transfer the plasmodium from the substratum on which you found it living to a piece of blotting paper which you can wet down in some near-by source of water. Should blotting paper not be available you can transport the plasmodium home by cutting away a part of the tree on which you found it. If you prefer you can raise your own plasmodium by merely taking home some of the reddish-brown powder and placing it on a damp and decayed piece of wood. Eventually the spores that emerge from the capillitium will germinate in the moisture and form the zoospores I mentioned above. These zoospores will swim about freely for a time and then come to rest when they form amœba-like bodies, which multiply by fission. Eventually they creep together in groups, and these in turn into larger groups until a new plasmodium is formed, completing the life cycle.

As you examine and study these peculiar and odd plants it may occur to you that they exhibit a number of animal characteristics, such as the locomotion of their amœboid plasmodia and the ingestion of solid food. This is true of course, indeed so true that some biologists regard them wholly as animals, and have given them the name of Mycetozoa, which means "the Fungus-animals." On the other hand, their sporangia and cellulose-walled spores are entirely plant-like, and it is for this reason that they are generally considered as plants. The group as a whole has no particular economic importance as far as man's interests are concerned, although one species does produce the damaging "club root" of cabbage.

We Are Intrigued by a Delightful Relationship

Those of us who pursue the study of Nature know that animals frequently associate together for some particular purpose. Sometimes the animals may be of the same species, such as zebras who herd together in large numbers for mutual protection; at other times the animals may be of different species. Such an instance, and one which to my mind is one of the most fascinating in the entire field of nature study, is the relationship between ants and plant-lice, or Aphids as they are also known.

The reason for the association between these two diverse forms of insect life lies in a liquid, sometimes referred to as honey-dew, which the Aphids secrete and which the ants are very fond of. If you can locate a colony of plant-lice, and you should have no difficulty in doing so for they are common enough, you may see, with the aid of a hand lens, the ants running about the plant-lice and patting them nervously with their antennæ until some Aphid finally responds by emitting from the end of the abdomen a glistening drop of watery fluid which the ant immediately snatches up. At one time it was believed that this fluid was furnished by the so-called honey-tubes, located on the back of the abdomen, but it is now known that it comes from the alimentary canal, the "honey-tubes" probably being repellent in function.

So well do the ants relish this fluid, that they will go to extreme lengths to preserve their source of supply. Not only do the ants protect the plant-lice from their natural enemies, but when autumn comes they collect the Aphid eggs and store them in their underground nests, preserving them over the winter as carefully as they do their own eggs. In spring they will prepare feeding grounds for the Aphids and then carry them there. Later they will transport them to other feeding grounds; and throughout the year exercise continual supervision over them. The plant-lice have been called "the milch cows of the ants," and I think the term is a very appropriate one indeed. Surely the ants take as much care of them as a farmer of his dairy herd, and for the same reason, to wit, for the liquid they furnish.

The plant-lice deserve our attention, not alone because of their interesting relationship to ants, but also because of their surprising life history. But before we go into that, let us examine one of them and see what they really look like. As you are quite aware these insects are rather small and so we find it necessary to examine them under the microscope. On doing so we find that the body is flask-shaped, that the wings have few veins, and that there is a three-jointed beak (Figure 133). You will also observe the two tubes on the back of the abdomen which at one time were supposed to secrete the "honey-dew" but which are now believed to be defensive weapons. As a rule Aphids are green in color, with a soft powdery bloom on the skin.

These insects are very numerous and this is because of the rapid rate at which they breed. Indeed, were it not for their innumerable natural enemies, they would probably destroy the greater part of plant life, for they are extremely destructive and prey upon practically all cultivated plants, from which they suck the juices. The rapidity in breeding is not due to extreme fertility as

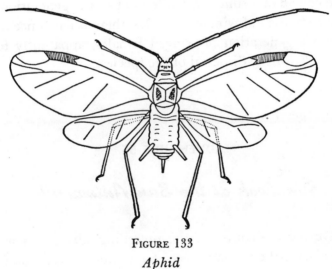

FIGURE 133
Aphid

the number of offspring of an individual female is rather small but rather to the early age at which the offspring themselves begin to reproduce. Now it so happens that the female offspring in order to reproduce do not need to be fertilized by males but can do so without their assistance, and furthermore do not lay eggs, but bring forth their young alive. In this way generation after generation is produced—as many as nine or ten—and so a single Aphid can become in one summer the parent of millions of children and grand-children. Eventually, however, there occurs a true sexual generation composed of males and females which pair, the females in this instance laying eggs instead of giving birth to living young. It is in this egg stage that the plant-lice usually pass the winter. Another peculiar feature in the life cycle of these insects is that during the course of a summer, while most of the generations are composed of wingless females, there occurs once or twice a generation of winged females, apparently to provide for the dispersal of the species.

ADVENTURE 55

We Look at the Sun Animalcule

During the course of the preceding adventures we have made the acquaintance of a number of very interesting microscopic animals that inhabit our fresh water ponds and pools, but we have yet to meet the Sun Animalcule or Actinophrys sol which appears to the naked eye as a whitish-grey spherical particle floating in the water or among the leaflets of aquatic plants. If we examine such a particle under the microscope, we will find that it seems to be composed of a collection of small bubbles, which are vacuoles, giving it a foamy appearance, and that it has numerous long, slender, pointed rods or rays radiating from the whole surface, the entire particle looking much like the pictures of

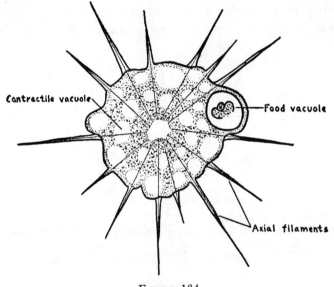

Contractile vacuole

Food vacuole

Axial filaments

FIGURE 134
Sun Animalcule

the sun found in almanacs, whence it derived its name (Figure 134).

The Sun Animalcule, which, as you may have guessed, is a unit mass of protoplasm like the Amœba, has practically no motion of its own, and for food must depend upon its rays or pseudopodia, which, as in the Amœba, are extensions of its own substance. The food consists of minute plants or animals, and when one of

213

these happens to come into contact with one of the rays it appears to adhere to it. Then, after a while, it glides down the pseudopodium until it reaches the central body where it is ingested after the fashion of the Amœba. If, however, the prey is large and vigorous enough to struggle to escape from the pseudopodium, other pseudopodia bend over and assist in the opera-tion of capture, much as the tentacles of Hydra may

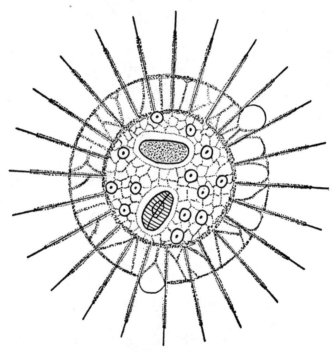

FIGURE 135
Actinosphærium Eichhorni

do, and then by their joint retractions convey the prey to the body where it is ingested. The struggles of such

214

animals and the ciliary action of smaller ones, such as Infusoria and Rotifers, may frequently be observed to continue even after they have been received into the body. Ultimately these movements cease, when digestion begins, the process being somewhat similar to that which takes place in the Amœba.

There is another animal which resembles the Sun Animalcule in appearance and which you may at first confuse with it. This species, which goes by the unpronounceable name of Actinosphærium Eichhorni (Figure 135) is larger in size, however, and is formed of an external layer of large vesicles or bubbles and a central mass of smaller protoplasmic bubbles. The rays, too, are different from those of the Sun Animalcule, being larger and coarser, and with a thread or fine rod-like filament running lengthwise through their middle and differing slightly in color from the softer part of the ray. To see these rays it will be necessary to use a higher power than that used in merely observing the animal.

ADVENTURE 56

We Approach the Science of Criminal Detection

In Adventure 12 I said something about the microscope being used in every day police work, in determining, for instance, whether a suspected blood stain is of blood or some other substance. Now the microscope is used by the police also for a number of other purposes, one of which is to supplement the Bertillon system * by identifying criminals and others by means of impressions left by the fingers.

If you press the tip of one of your fingers upon a metal surface covered with a thin film of printer's ink, and then upon a paper or card, you will have an impression of the ridges and furrows of that particular finger. Such ridges and furrows remain unchanged through life and cannot be altered by cuts, burns, in fact by any known means. Moreover, it has been estimated that the variations are so great that the chance of identity between two single prints are only one in sixty-four billion. On a comparison of ten digits, identification is said to be absolute.

Now the patterns of the skin may be classified under three types—the arch, the loop and the whorl types. In all instances the papillary ridges run across the fingers in the vicinity of the third joint, and at the tip they follow the curve of the nail in the rounded arch. In some cases, the ridges between follow the outer ones in a more or less even arch of lessening convexity as shown in Figure 136A. This pattern is known as the arch type. In the loop type, the intermediate ridges form a loop running from one side inward to the center of the tip and then doubling back and at the opposite side of the finger the outer ridges, the loop, and the basal ridges between them form a triangle known as

* *A system for the identification of persons by a physical description based upon anthropometric measurements, notes of markings, deformities, color, impressions of thumb lines, etc.*

the delta (Figure 136B). Finally in the third type, the ridges on the tip may be so twisted as to form a complete circle, cutting off two deltas, as shown in Figure 136C.

These three types of patterns serve only as a primary division in the classification of finger prints, for certain combinations of these digital formulæ are much more common than others, and thus necessitate further subdivisions. This is done by studying the minuter struc-

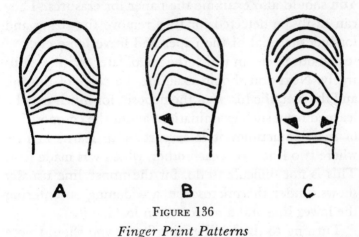

A   **B**   **C**

FIGURE 136
Finger Print Patterns

tures of the finger-print, and particularly by counting the ridges in the loops of those fingers which show that structure. This is where the microscope comes in, for such details cannot very well be discerned with the naked eye. You will find on examining finger-prints that only a magnification of ten or twenty diameters is needed and you should therefore use your lowest objective.

Frequently the microscope is an important legal aid

in determining whether or not a certain document has been tampered with or whether a certain signature is a forgery. You may never have occasion to use your microscope for either of these purposes but it is just as well to know how, should the need ever arise.

First of all, you should examine the paper of the document in question to learn of what material it is made; then its texture and sizing and its water-mark, for such information is frequently of great importance. You should also examine the paper for erasures. They can easily be detected for they remove the sizing and loading material of the paper and leave loose ends of teased-out fibers, in which the ink of later writings runs freely. Next you should examine the color of the ink and the metallic luster of the deposit, for much may be learned from such examinations about the composition of inks. Sometimes it is important to learn, in case where two lines cross each other, which was made first. This is not difficult to do, for the upper line usually shows, under the microscope, a widening on entering the lower line and a narrower on leaving it.

Turning to the handwriting itself, you should note the general spacing of the lines, words and letters, and observe more carefully the pen pressure, the shading, and the general symmetry of words and letters, for all these are significant as indicating something of the temperament and make-up of the writer.

We must point out that the more obvious peculiarities can easily be imitated by real skill and it is only by the more minute characteristics, as shown by the microscope, that certain identification of handwriting is possible. One of such characteristics is that long lines exhibit certain variations of direction, these variations in number and nature differing according to the writer. A second is that much finer fluctuations occur in the shape of vertical deviations from side to side and changes in width due to periodic changes in the pressure of the penpoint. And a third is that on one or both margins of the line there are still more minute lateral serrations. All of these characteristics are necessarily influenced to some extent by the paper and writing instrument as well as by the physical and mental condition of the writer, but nevertheless they vary so markedly with different individuals that they are usually a reliable guide to the identity of the handwriting.

ADVENTURE 57

We Solve a Mystery

On the leaves of such plants as the lilac and the rambler roses, a delicate, grayish, mold-like or cobweb-like coating, looking for all the world like a film of dried soap suds, may sometimes be seen. Perhaps such coatings may have been a source of much mystery to you. If so, we can easily solve the mystery. All that you have to do is to examine some of the coating under the microscope to find it to be the branching mycelium of a fungus which spreads over the surface of the leaf. From this mycelium you should find short hyphæ extending down into the tissues of the leaf (Figure 137). These hyphæ are called haustoria, (singular, haustorium) and their purpose is to absorb from the leaf the

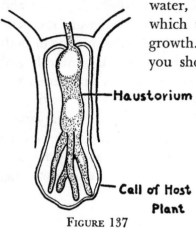

water, mineral salts and food which the fungus requires for growth. From this mycelium you should also find short hyphæ extending vertically upward from the leaf and bearing spores, which are developed one at a time by cell division of the end of the hyphæ (Figure 138). Spores formed in this manner are known as conidia.

FIGURE 137

Haustorium of Powdery Mildew

Such spores readily break apart from one another, and, being microscopic in size, are disseminated by the wind. On reaching a film of water on some other plant, they germinate into mycelia, which in turn produce haustoria and conidia and thus repeat the life cycle on a new host.

In autumn, minute black spots, each smaller than the point of a lead pencil, may be seen amidst the grayish mycelium. Under the microscope these spots will appear as hard black spheres from which hyphæ radiate like the spokes of a wheel (Figure 139) and each of which ends in a hook of characteristic form. The spheres are known as perithecia, and if you break one open you will find it to contain one or several thin-walled sacs, called asci, and, lying free from one another within each sac, two to eight ellipsoidal cells. These cells are spores, and are known as ascospores.

The formation of the perithecia is the plant's way of surviving through the winter, for it can grow on nothing but living plants. Thus in the autumn, when the leaves fall and the mycelium dies, the perithecia and their contents continue to live through the protection of their heavy walls. In the following spring, when subjected to moisture, the perithecia crack open, freeing the asci, which in turn rupture and release the ascospores. On finding the proper host, for the fungus can infect only certain kinds of host plants, the ascospores germinate into new mycelia, and thus a new cycle is begun.

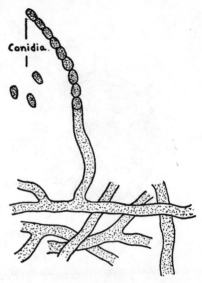

FIGURE 138

Conidia of Powdery Mildew

There are some hundred different species of the fungus plant which we have just examined; and collectively the group is known as the Powdery Mildews, from the powder-like appearance of the black perithecia.

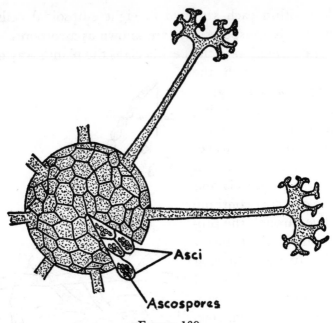

Asci

Ascospores

FIGURE 139
Perithecium of Powdery Mildew

ADVENTURE 58

We Observe a Wonderful Provision of Nature

It is a rule of Nature, and a rule to which there are no exceptions, that every living thing must ultimately die. Why the vital machine that maintains the life of an individual should wear out is a mystery that has tormented the mind of man ever since he began to think, but that it has definite implications is shown by the fact that the span of natural life varies with the species.

Now it is not our intention to enter into a philosophical or scientific discussion on the mystery of life; our only excuse for beginning this adventure as we did is to have a starting point from which we can go on to say that since every living thing must eventually die, life must soon perish from the face of the earth if no provision were made for all living things to reproduce their kind. That such a provision has been made we all know, and in the preceding adventures we have seen instances of it. This ability of living things to reproduce their kind, by detaching from themselves parts or fragments possessing the power of growth and development and leading in turn to further continuance of the life cycle, is unquestionably the most remarkable and intriguing of all natural phenomena.

The simplest method by which a species can reproduce its kind is by dividing in two, as in the Amœba. The next simplest method is that by which masses of cells may become detached from the body and give rise to offspring, as in the budding of Hydra. Such reproduction, when the detached portion (which may be either a simple cell or a group of cells) has the power of developing into a new individual without the influence of other living matter, is known as asexual reproduction, in contrast to sexual reproduction, in which the detached portion (in this instance always a single cell, *ovum*) must be acted upon by the detached portion (likewise a single cell, *sperm*) from another individual before it can develop into a new individual, the union of the two being known as fertilization. Such a method of reproduction we have become acquainted with in our study of the higher plants. (See Adventure 47.)

Among the animals that reproduce by the sexual method, the common earthworm provides us with an

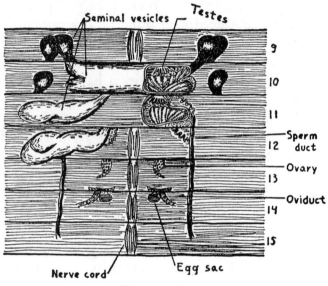

FIGURE 140
Reproductive System of Earthworm

easy means of examining the various structures that are employed in the process; and I am quite sure that you will be interested in seeing what they look like.

Our first step is to obtain one of these animals. The best time to do so is on a warm, rainy night when the earthworms may be found extended on the surface of the ground from their burrows. They may also be found on cloudy days after a prolonged hard rain and in the winter nearly always under manure piles. Try to obtain one of the large species, which can be recognized by its flattened posterior end.

On returning home, place your live worm in a flat dish of water and pour on sufficient water to cover it. Then add a little alcohol from time to time until the strength of the liquid is increased to about ten per cent. Next wash all the mucous from the body and replace it in the ten per cent alcohol solution until it no longer responds to pricking or pinching with your forceps. Then transfer it to fifty per cent alcohol, in which you leave it for several hours. At the end of this time it will be ready for dissection. With a small scissors cut it open, from the anterior to the posterior end, a trifle to one side of the mid-dorsal line. Then a general view of the internal structure may be obtained.

At this point I must warn you that both male and female sexual organs occur in the earthworm and are not separate as in other animals. So do not get excited and think that you have found a freak of Nature. The female system consists essentially of a pair of ovaries and a pair of oviducts. The ovaries, in which the eggs arise, are pear-shaped in form and are located in the thirteenth segment, where they lie on either side of the central nerve cord and attached by their broader end, as shown in the diagram (Figure 140). The oviducts, which serve to conduct the eggs to the exterior, are two short trumpet-shaped tubes lying immediately posterior to the ovaries. They open into the thirteenth segment by a wide ciliated funnel, and pass into the fourteenth segment, where they enlarge into an egg sac, and then open to the exterior. In the egg sac, the eggs taken up by the funnel are temporarily stored before passing out.

The male system consists essentially of two pairs of testes, two sperm ducts (vasa deferentia), and three pairs of seminal vesicles. The testes, in outward appearance somewhat similar to the ovaries, are small, glove-shaped bodies lying one on either side of the nerve cord in segments ten and eleven, and it is in them that the sperm cells, or spermatozoa as they are usually called, arise. The sperm ducts, which serve to conduct the spermatozoa to the exterior, are very long slender tubes open like the oviducts at both ends. The outer opening is a conspicuous slit on the ventral side of the fifteenth segment. From this point the duct runs forward to the twelfth segment, where it branches like a Y, one end of the two branches terminating in the eleventh segment, the other in the tenth. The end of each of these branches, after twisting into a peculiar knot, terminates in a ciliated funnel immediately posterior to the respective testes, and their function is, of course, to take up the spermatozoa. I might add here, in case you have difficulty in finding the testes and sperm funnels, that they can readily be made out only in the young specimens. In mature worms they are completely enveloped by the seminal vesicles, which are perhaps the most conspicuous part of the entire reproductive apparatus. These may be recognized as the large white bodies or pouches lying in segments nine to twelve. In the cavities of these vesicles the spermatozoa which leave the testes at a very early period float freely and pass many stages of their development, until they become mature, when they pass into the funnels of the sperm ducts.

Having found the various reproductive structures, our next step is to dissect an ovary, employing for this purpose a pair of forceps and a small curved scissors. We stain it in borax carmine, then dehydrate and mount it on a slide in a little Canada balsam. On viewing it through the microscope we will find it to be a most beautiful object. We repeat this process with one of the testes.

Since an individual earthworm produces both the sperm and egg cells, it might seem that the sexual union of two different individuals would not be necessary. This, however, is not the case for the sperm cells must be transferred from one worm to another, this taking place during a process called copulation. When copulation is about to occur, two worms come together and, placing themselves so that their heads point in opposite directions, secrete a cocoon around the saddle-shaped enlargement known as the clitellum and easily seen on the exterior of the animal. Into the cocoon eggs and spermatozoa are deposited; whereupon the cocoon is then gradually worked forward toward the head of the worm by contractions of the body. As the cocoon passes off, the open ends immediately contract tightly together and the cocoon becomes a closed capsule containing both eggs and spermatozoa. Fertilization of the eggs now takes place and embryological development begins, until finally a young earthworm is formed. It breaks through the walls of the capsule and makes its entry into the world.

ADVENTURE 59

We See What Makes Animals "Go"

Since we started out on our first adventure, we have become acquainted with a number of animals, and with a number of plants, some strange and some not so strange. We have learned things about these animals and plants that most of us did not know, and we have learned how many of them perform the necessary activities essential to their existence. We have seen how plants make their own food and grow and reproduce. We have seen how animals feed and how they digest their food; how they reproduce their kind and how they breathe. In fact we have gained an insight into all the activities that go on within an animal but we have still one more thing to do—to examine that part of the animal without which it could not perform any of its activities. You have guessed it; it is the nerv-

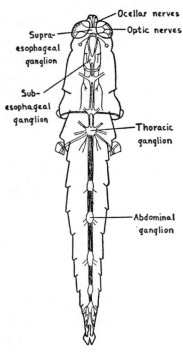

Labels: Ocellar nerves, Optic nerves, Supra-esophageal ganglion, Sub-esophageal ganglion, Thoracic ganglion, Abdominal ganglion

FIGURE 141

Nervous System of Grass-hopper

228

ous system, that intricate pattern of nerves and fibers that permits an animal to see, to move, to eat; in other words to perform all the essential activities necessary to maintain life.

The nervous system we shall examine is that of the grasshopper. The reason for our choice is that in this insect it is somewhat simple in structure and therefore fairly easy to examine.

The nervous system of the grasshopper consists of a series of nerve-centers, or ganglia, extending along the median line of the floor of the body, each of which is connected by two cords (commissures). The two cords in some insects are united into one in some parts of the body (Figure 141). In the grasshopper, there are ten of these nerve-centers or ganglia, two in the head, three in the thorax, and five in the abdomen. The first ganglion (singular of ganglia) is somewhat larger than the others, and is called the "brain," or supra-esophageal ganglion from the fact that it rests upon the esophagus. From this ganglion, or "brain," arise large, short optic nerves which go to the compound eyes, three slender filaments which are sent to the three ocelli,* and others that go to the antennæ.

The second ganglion, known as the subesophageal because it lies under the esophagus at the base of the head and directly behind the tongue, is connected with the "brain" by two commissures passing up each side of the esophagus. From the under side of this ganglion

* The ocelli, which are commonly three in number, are simple eyes and supplementary to the compound ones. They are designed to form images of objects at close range or simply to distinguish between light and darkness, whereas the compound eyes, such as we found in the house fly, are adapted to perceive form and movements.

arise three pairs of nerves, which are distributed to the mandibles, maxillæ, and labium.

In addition to these ganglia, there are a number of others which collectively are known as the sympathetic system. This system is apparent in a recurrent nerve which, arising in a frontal ganglion and terminating in a stomachic ganglion situated at the anterior end of the mid-intestine, lies along the median dorsal line of the esophagus. With it are connected two pairs of lateral ganglia (Figure 142). Finally in some insects the ventral nerve cord may include also a median nerve thread, from which extend paired nerves to the muscles of the spiracles.

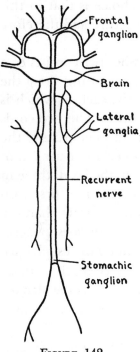

FIGURE 142

Diagram of Sympathetic Nervous System

All this may seem like Greek to you but when you examine the nervous system under the microscope it should become much clearer. In order to examine it, however, we must first dissect it from the body. Our first step is to cut the insect open and to remove the alimentary canal. When you have done this I think you will recognize the nervous system from my description and the diagram (Figure 142). I am afraid that in order to remove it from the body you will have to use a hand lens so as to see what you are doing; and I am also afraid that you might find it a somewhat ticklish operation. However, persevere and when you have at last removed it, wash it in water and stain with borax carmine. Then mount on a slide and examine under the microscope.

The function of the various ganglia which go to make up the nervous system is somewhat as follows: the "brain" innervates the chief sensory organs, which are the eyes and antennæ, and converts such sensory stimuli as it may receive into motor stimuli; which in turn effect co-ordinated muscular or other movements in response to particular sensations from the environment. In other words, it directs the locomotor movements of the legs and wings. Thus, for instance, if the insect should be deprived of its "brain," it is unable to go to its food, and it will walk or fly in an erratic manner, showing that it lacks co-ordination of muscular action.

The sub-esophageal ganglion controls the mouth parts, while the thoracic ganglia govern the appendages of their respective segments. The thoracic ganglia, as well as those of the abdomen, are more or less independent of "brain" control, each of them being an individual motor center for its particular segment. Proof of this is shown by the fact that if the insect is decapitated it may still continue to breathe, walk or fly—for a limited time, of course.

As for the sympathetic system, the anterior ganglion governs the swallowing movements; the dorsal sympathetic system controls the dorsal vessel * and the sali-

* See Adventure 33 for dorsal vessel.

231

vary glands; and the ventral system operates the spiracular muscles.

For the reception of sensory impressions, the skin or integument of insects has become modified in a number of ways, such modifications being known as sense organs or end-organs. Usually they are the most numerous and varied on the head and its appendages, especially the antennæ, but they may occur on almost any part of the body, and are classified as to touch, taste, and smell. Touch end-organs are bristles or hairs, which are connected with a nerve. Do not get the idea that all the hairs of an insect are sensory, for this is not so; only those connected with a nerve are sensory, and such hairs are more commonly found in such appendages as the antennæ, palpi and cerci.* The end-organs of taste may be minute setæ, but more commonly pegs, each seated in a pit, or cup, and connected with a nerve fiber. In the Honey Bee, as I pointed out in Adventure 51, the taste organs may be found as short setæ on the tongue, and in the common Yellow Jacket Wasp as pits on the maxillæ, each with a cone, or pit, projecting from its base. Lastly, the end-organs of smell are usually apparent also as pegs, or perhaps as bristles, and in some instances they take the form of teeth or cones projecting from the surface of the antennæ, as in the common Yellow Jacket. You can see all of this for yourself if you will examine under the microscope the tongue of the bee and the maxillæ and antennæ of the wasp.

* In the male grasshoppers the cerci are a pair of appendages at the extremity of the abdomen and serve to hold the female during copulation.

A CATALOGUE OF SELECTED DOVER BOOKS
IN ALL FIELDS OF INTEREST

A CATALOGUE OF SELECTED DOVER BOOKS
IN ALL FIELDS OF INTEREST

LEATHER TOOLING AND CARVING, Chris H. Groneman. One of few books concentrating on tooling and carving, with complete instructions and grid designs for 39 projects ranging from bookmarks to bags. 148 illustrations. 111pp. 7⅞ x 10.
23061-9 Pa. $2.50

THE CODEX NUTTALL, A PICTURE MANUSCRIPT FROM ANCIENT MEXICO, as first edited by Zelia Nuttall. Only inexpensive edition, in full color, of a pre-Columbian Mexican (Mixtec) book. 88 color plates show kings, gods, heroes, temples, sacrifices. New explanatory, historical introduction by Arthur G. Miller. 96pp. 11⅜ x 8½.
23168-2 Pa. $7.50

AMERICAN PRIMITIVE PAINTING, Jean Lipman. Classic collection of an enduring American tradition. 109 plates, 8 in full color—portraits, landscapes, Biblical and historical scenes, etc., showing family groups, farm life, and so on. 80pp. of lucid text. 8⅜ x 11¼.
22815-0 Pa. $4.00

WILL BRADLEY: HIS GRAPHIC ART, edited by Clarence P. Hornung. Striking collection of work by foremost practitioner of Art Nouveau in America: posters, cover designs, sample pages, advertisements, other illustrations. 97 plates, including 8 in full color and 19 in two colors. 97pp. 9⅜ x 12¼.
20701-3 Pa. $4.00
22120-2 Clothbd. $10.00

THE UNDERGROUND SKETCHBOOK OF JAN FAUST, Jan Faust. 101 bitter, horrifying, black-humorous, penetrating sketches on sex, war, greed, various liberations, etc. Sometimes sexual, but not pornographic. Not for prudish. 101pp. 6½ x 9¼.
22740-5 Pa. $1.50

THE GIBSON GIRL AND HER AMERICA, Charles Dana Gibson. 155 finest drawings of effervescent world of 1900-1910: the Gibson Girl and her loves, amusements, adventures, Mr. Pipp, etc. Selected by E. Gillon; introduction by Henry Pitz. 144pp. 8¼ x 11⅜.
21986-0 Pa. $3.50

STAINED GLASS CRAFT, J.A.F. Divine, G. Blachford. One of the very few books that tell the beginner exactly what he needs to know: planning cuts, making shapes, avoiding design weaknesses, fitting glass, etc. 93 illustrations. 115pp.
22812-6 Pa. $1.50

CREATIVE LITHOGRAPHY AND HOW TO DO IT, Grant Arnold. Lithography as art form: working directly on stone, transfer of drawings, lithotint, mezzotint, color printing; also metal plates. Detailed, thorough. 27 illustrations. 214pp.
21208-4 Pa. $3.00

DESIGN MOTIFS OF ANCIENT MEXICO, Jorge Enciso. Vigorous, powerful ceramic stamp impressions — Maya, Aztec, Toltec, Olmec. Serpents, gods, priests, dancers, etc. 153pp. 6⅛ x 9¼. 20084-1 Pa. $2.50

AMERICAN INDIAN DESIGN AND DECORATION, Leroy Appleton. Full text, plus more than 700 precise drawings of Inca, Maya, Aztec, Pueblo, Plains, NW Coast basketry, sculpture, painting, pottery, sand paintings, metal, etc. 4 plates in color. 279pp. 8⅜ x 11¼. 22704-9 Pa. $4.50

CHINESE LATTICE DESIGNS, Daniel S. Dye. Incredibly beautiful geometric designs: circles, voluted, simple dissections, etc. Inexhaustible source of ideas, motifs. 1239 illustrations. 469pp. 6⅛ x 9¼. 23096-1 Pa. $5.00

JAPANESE DESIGN MOTIFS, Matsuya Co. Mon, or heraldic designs. Over 4000 typical, beautiful designs: birds, animals, flowers, swords, fans, geometric; all beautifully stylized. 213pp. 11⅜ x 8¼. 22874-6 Pa. $5.00

PERSPECTIVE, Jan Vredeman de Vries. 73 perspective plates from 1604 edition; buildings, townscapes, stairways, fantastic scenes. Remarkable for beauty, surrealistic atmosphere; real eye-catchers. Introduction by Adolf Placzek. 74pp. 11⅜ x 8¼. 20186-4 Pa. $2.75

EARLY AMERICAN DESIGN MOTIFS, Suzanne E. Chapman. 497 motifs, designs, from painting on wood, ceramics, appliqué, glassware, samplers, metal work, etc. Florals, landscapes, birds and animals, geometrics, letters, etc. Inexhaustible. Enlarged edition. 138pp. 8⅜ x 11¼. 22985-8 Pa. $3.50
23084-8 Clothbd. $7.95

VICTORIAN STENCILS FOR DESIGN AND DECORATION, edited by E.V. Gillon, Jr. 113 wonderful ornate Victorian pieces from German sources; florals, geometrics; borders, corner pieces; bird motifs, etc. 64pp. 9⅜ x 12¼. 21995-X Pa. $2.75

ART NOUVEAU: AN ANTHOLOGY OF DESIGN AND ILLUSTRATION FROM THE STUDIO, edited by E.V. Gillon, Jr. Graphic arts: book jackets, posters, engravings, illustrations, decorations; Crane, Beardsley, Bradley and many others. Inexhaustible. 92pp. 8⅛ x 11. 22388-4 Pa. $2.50

ORIGINAL ART DECO DESIGNS, William Rowe. First-rate, highly imaginative modern Art Deco frames, borders, compositions, alphabets, florals, insectals, Wurlitzer-types, etc. Much finest modern Art Deco. 80 plates, 8 in color. 8⅜ x 11¼. 22567-4 Pa. $3.00

HANDBOOK OF DESIGNS AND DEVICES, Clarence P. Hornung. Over 1800 basic geometric designs based on circle, triangle, square, scroll, cross, etc. Largest such collection in existence. 261pp. 20125-2 Pa. $2.50

150 MASTERPIECES OF DRAWING, edited by Anthony Toney. 150 plates, early 15th century to end of 18th century; Rembrandt, Michelangelo, Dürer, Fragonard, Watteau, Wouwerman, many others. 150pp. 8⅜ x 11¼.   21032-4 Pa. $3.50

THE GOLDEN AGE OF THE POSTER, Hayward and Blanche Cirker. 70 extraordinary posters in full colors, from Maîtres de l'Affiche, Mucha, Lautrec, Bradley, Cheret, Beardsley, many others. 9⅜ x 12¼.   22753-7 Pa. $4.95
21718-3 Clothbd. $7.95

SIMPLICISSIMUS, selection, translations and text by Stanley Appelbaum. 180 satirical drawings, 16 in full color, from the famous German weekly magazine in the years 1896 to 1926. 24 artists included: Grosz, Kley, Pascin, Kubin, Kollwitz, plus Heine, Thöny, Bruno Paul, others. 172pp. 8½ x 12¼.   23098-8 Pa. $5.00
23099-6 Clothbd. $10.00

THE EARLY WORK OF AUBREY BEARDSLEY, Aubrey Beardsley. 157 plates, 2 in color: Manon Lescaut, Madame Bovary, Morte d'Arthur, Salome, other. Introduction by H. Marillier. 175pp. 8½ x 11.   21816-3 Pa. $3.50

THE LATER WORK OF AUBREY BEARDSLEY, Aubrey Beardsley. Exotic masterpieces of full maturity: Venus and Tannhäuser, Lysistrata, Rape of the Lock, Volpone, Savoy material, etc. 174 plates, 2 in color. 176pp. 8½ x 11.   21817-1 Pa. $4.00

DRAWINGS OF WILLIAM BLAKE, William Blake. 92 plates from Book of Job, Divine Comedy, Paradise Lost, visionary heads, mythological figures, Laocoön, etc. Selection, introduction, commentary by Sir Geoffrey Keynes. 178pp. 8½ x 11.
22303-5 Pa. $3.50

LONDON: A PILGRIMAGE, Gustave Doré, Blanchard Jerrold. Squalor, riches, misery, beauty of mid-Victorian metropolis; 55 wonderful plates, 125 other illustrations, full social, cultural text by Jerrold. 191pp. of text. 8⅛ x 11.
22306-X Pa. $5.00

THE COMPLETE WOODCUTS OF ALBRECHT DÜRER, edited by Dr. W. Kurth. 346 in all: Old Testament, St. Jerome, Passion, Life of Virgin, Apocalypse, many others. Introduction by Campbell Dodgson. 285pp. 8½ x 12¼.   21097-9 Pa. $6.00

THE DISASTERS OF WAR, Francisco Goya. 83 etchings record horrors of Napoleonic wars in Spain and war in general. Reprint of 1st edition, plus 3 additional plates. Introduction by Philip Hofer. 97pp. 9⅜ x 8¼.   21872-4 Pa. $3.00

ENGRAVINGS OF HOGARTH, William Hogarth. 101 of Hogarth's greatest works: Rake's Progress, Harlot's Progress, Illustrations for Hudibras, Midnight Modern Conversation, Before and After, Beer Street and Gin Lane, many more. Full commentary. 256pp. 11 x 14.   22479-1 Pa. $7.00
23023-6 Clothbd. $13.50

PRIMITIVE ART, Franz Boas. Great anthropologist on ceramics, textiles, wood, stone, metal, etc.; patterns, technology, symbols, styles. All areas, but fullest on Northwest Coast Indians. 350 illustrations. 378pp.   20025-6 Pa. $3.50

MOTHER GOOSE'S MELODIES. Facsimile of fabulously rare Munroe and Francis "copyright 1833" Boston edition. Familiar and unusual rhymes, wonderful old woodcut illustrations. Edited by E.F. Bleiler. 128pp. 4½ x 6⅜. 22577-1 Pa. $1.00

MOTHER GOOSE IN HIEROGLYPHICS. Favorite nursery rhymes presented in rebus form for children. Fascinating 1849 edition reproduced in toto, with key. Introduction by E.F. Bleiler. About 400 woodcuts. 64pp. 6⅞ x 5¼. 20745-5 Pa. $1.00

PETER PIPER'S PRACTICAL PRINCIPLES OF PLAIN & PERFECT PRONUNCIATION. Alliterative jingles and tongue-twisters. Reproduction in full of 1830 first American edition. 25 spirited woodcuts. 32pp. 4½ x 6⅜. 22560-7 Pa. $1.00

MARMADUKE MULTIPLY'S MERRY METHOD OF MAKING MINOR MATHEMATICIANS. Fellow to Peter Piper, it teaches multiplication table by catchy rhymes and woodcuts. 1841 Munroe & Francis edition. Edited by E.F. Bleiler. 103pp. 4⅝ x 6.
22773-1 Pa. $1.25
20171-6 Clothbd. $3.00

THE NIGHT BEFORE CHRISTMAS, Clement Moore. Full text, and woodcuts from original 1848 book. Also critical, historical material. 19 illustrations. 40pp. 4⅝ x 6. 22797-9 Pa. $1.00

THE KING OF THE GOLDEN RIVER, John Ruskin. Victorian children's classic of three brothers, their attempts to reach the Golden River, what becomes of them. Facsimile of original 1889 edition. 22 illustrations. 56pp. 4⅝ x 6⅜.
20066-3 Pa. $1.25

DREAMS OF THE RAREBIT FIEND, Winsor McCay. Pioneer cartoon strip, unexcelled for beauty, imagination, in 60 full sequences. Incredible technical virtuosity, wonderful visual wit. Historical introduction. 62pp. 8⅜ x 11¼. 21347-1 Pa. $2.50

THE KATZENJAMMER KIDS, Rudolf Dirks. In full color, 14 strips from 1906-7; full of imagination, characteristic humor. Classic of great historical importance. Introduction by August Derleth. 32pp. 9¼ x 12¼. 23005-8 Pa. $2.00

LITTLE ORPHAN ANNIE AND LITTLE ORPHAN ANNIE IN COSMIC CITY, Harold Gray. Two great sequences from the early strips: our curly-haired heroine defends the Warbucks' financial empire and, then, takes on meanie Phineas P. Pinchpenny. Leapin' lizards! 178pp. 6⅛ x 8⅜. 23107-0 Pa. $2.00

WHEN A FELLER NEEDS A FRIEND, Clare Briggs. 122 cartoons by one of the greatest newspaper cartoonists of the early 20th century — about growing up, making a living, family life, daily frustrations and occasional triumphs. 121pp. 8½ x 9½.
23148-8 Pa. $2.50

THE BEST OF GLUYAS WILLIAMS. 100 drawings by one of America's finest cartoonists: The Day a Cake of Ivory Soap Sank at Proctor & Gamble's, At the Life Insurance Agents' Banquet, and many other gems from the 20's and 30's. 118pp. 8⅜ x 11¼. 22737-5 Pa. $2.50

THE BEST DR. THORNDYKE DETECTIVE STORIES, R. Austin Freeman. The Case of Oscar Brodski, The Moabite Cipher, and 5 other favorites featuring the great scientific detective, plus his long-believed-lost first adventure — 31 New Inn — reprinted here for the first time. Edited by E.F. Bleiler. USO 20388-3 Pa. $3.00

BEST "THINKING MACHINE" DETECTIVE STORIES, Jacques Futrelle. The Problem of Cell 13 and 11 other stories about Prof. Augustus S.F.X. Van Dusen, including two "lost" stories. First reprinting of several. Edited by E.F. Bleiler. 241pp. 20537-1 Pa. $3.00

UNCLE SILAS, J. Sheridan LeFanu. Victorian Gothic mystery novel, considered by many best of period, even better than Collins or Dickens. Wonderful psychological terror. Introduction by Frederick Shroyer. 436pp.   21715-9 Pa. $4.00

BEST DR. POGGIOLI DETECTIVE STORIES, T.S. Stribling. 15 best stories from EQMM and The Saint offer new adventures in Mexico, Florida, Tennessee hills as Poggioli unravels mysteries and combats Count Jalacki. 217pp.   23227-1 Pa. $3.00

EIGHT DIME NOVELS, selected with an introduction by E.F. Bleiler. Adventures of Old King Brady, Frank James, Nick Carter, Deadwood Dick, Buffalo Bill, The Steam Man, Frank Merriwell, and Horatio Alger — 1877 to 1905. Important, entertaining popular literature in facsimile reprint, with original covers. 190pp. 9 x 12.   22975-0 Pa. $3.50

ALICE'S ADVENTURES UNDER GROUND, Lewis Carroll. Facsimile of ms. Carroll gave Alice Liddell in 1864. Different in many ways from final Alice. Handlettered, illustrated by Carroll. Introduction by Martin Gardner. 128pp. 21482-6 Pa. $1.50

ALICE IN WONDERLAND COLORING BOOK, Lewis Carroll. Pictures by John Tenniel. Large-size versions of the famous illustrations of Alice, Cheshire Cat, Mad Hatter and all the others, waiting for your crayons. Abridged text. 36 illustrations. 64pp. 8¼ x 11.   22853-3 Pa. $1.50

AVENTURES D'ALICE AU PAYS DES MERVEILLES, Lewis Carroll. Bué's translation of "Alice" into French, supervised by Carroll himself. Novel way to learn language. (No English text.) 42 Tenniel illustrations. 196pp.   22836-3 Pa. $2.50

MYTHS AND FOLK TALES OF IRELAND, Jeremiah Curtin. 11 stories that are Irish versions of European fairy tales and 9 stories from the Fenian cycle — 20 tales of legend and magic that comprise an essential work in the history of folklore. 256pp.   22430-9 Pa. $3.00

EAST O' THE SUN AND WEST O' THE MOON, George W. Dasent. Only full edition of favorite, wonderful Norwegian fairytales — Why the Sea is Salt, Boots and the Troll, etc. — with 77 illustrations by Kittelsen & Werenskiöld. 418pp.   22521-6 Pa. $4.00

PERRAULT'S FAIRY TALES, Charles Perrault and Gustave Doré. Original versions of Cinderella, Sleeping Beauty, Little Red Riding Hood, etc. in best translation, with 34 wonderful illustrations by Gustave Doré. 117pp. 8⅛ x 11.   22311-6 Pa. $2.50

EARLY NEW ENGLAND GRAVESTONE RUBBINGS, Edmund V. Gillon, Jr. 43 photographs, 226 rubbings show heavily symbolic, macabre, sometimes humorous primitive American art. Up to early 19th century. 207pp. 8⅜ x 11¼.
21380-3 Pa. $4.00

L.J.M. DAGUERRE: THE HISTORY OF THE DIORAMA AND THE DAGUERREOTYPE, Helmut and Alison Gernsheim. Definitive account. Early history, life and work of Daguerre; discovery of daguerreotype process; diffusion abroad; other early photography. 124 illustrations. 226pp. 6⅙ x 9¼.
22290-X Pa. $4.00

PHOTOGRAPHY AND THE AMERICAN SCENE, Robert Taft. The basic book on American photography as art, recording form, 1839-1889. Development, influence on society, great photographers, types (portraits, war, frontier, etc.), whatever else needed. Inexhaustible. Illustrated with 322 early photos, daguerreotypes, tintypes, stereo slides, etc. 546pp. 6⅛ x 9¼.
21201-7 Pa. $5.95

PHOTOGRAPHIC SKETCHBOOK OF THE CIVIL WAR, Alexander Gardner. Reproduction of 1866 volume with 100 on-the-field photographs: Manassas, Lincoln on battlefield, slave pens, etc. Introduction by E.F. Bleiler. 224pp. 10¾ x 9.
22731-6 Pa. $5.00

THE MOVIES: A PICTURE QUIZ BOOK, Stanley Appelbaum & Hayward Cirker. Match stars with their movies, name actors and actresses, test your movie skill with 241 stills from 236 great movies, 1902-1959. Indexes of performers and films. 128pp. 8⅜ x 9¼.
20222-4 Pa. $2.50

THE TALKIES, Richard Griffith. Anthology of features, articles from Photoplay, 1928-1940, reproduced complete. Stars, famous movies, technical features, fabulous ads, etc.; Garbo, Chaplin, King Kong, Lubitsch, etc. 4 color plates, scores of illustrations. 327pp. 8⅜ x 11¼.
22762-6 Pa. $6.95

THE MOVIE MUSICAL FROM VITAPHONE TO "42ND STREET," edited by Miles Kreuger. Relive the rise of the movie musical as reported in the pages of Photoplay magazine (1926-1933): every movie review, cast list, ad, and record review; every significant feature article, production still, biography, forecast, and gossip story. Profusely illustrated. 367pp. 8⅜ x 11¼.
23154-2 Pa. $6.95

JOHANN SEBASTIAN BACH, Philipp Spitta. Great classic of biography, musical commentary, with hundreds of pieces analyzed. Also good for Bach's contemporaries. 450 musical examples. Total of 1799pp.
EUK 22278-0, 22279-9 Clothbd., Two vol. set $25.00

BEETHOVEN AND HIS NINE SYMPHONIES, Sir George Grove. Thorough history, analysis, commentary on symphonies and some related pieces. For either beginner or advanced student. 436 musical passages. 407pp.
20334-4 Pa. $4.00

MOZART AND HIS PIANO CONCERTOS, Cuthbert Girdlestone. The only full-length study. Detailed analyses of all 21 concertos, sources; 417 musical examples. 509pp.
21271-8 Pa. $4.50

THE FITZWILLIAM VIRGINAL BOOK, edited by J. Fuller Maitland, W.B. Squire. Famous early 17th century collection of keyboard music, 300 works by Morley, Byrd, Bull, Gibbons, etc. Modern notation. Total of 938pp. 8⅜ x 11.
ECE 21068-5, 21069-3 Pa., Two vol. set $14.00

COMPLETE STRING QUARTETS, Wolfgang A. Mozart. Breitkopf and Härtel edition. All 23 string quartets plus alternate slow movement to K156. Study score. 277pp. 9⅜ x 12¼.
22372-8 Pa. $6.00

COMPLETE SONG CYCLES, Franz Schubert. Complete piano, vocal music of Die Schöne Müllerin, Die Winterreise, Schwanengesang. Also Drinker English singing translations. Breitkopf and Härtel edition. 217pp. 9⅜ x 12¼.
22649-2 Pa. $4.50

THE COMPLETE PRELUDES AND ETUDES FOR PIANOFORTE SOLO, Alexander Scriabin. All the preludes and etudes including many perfectly spun miniatures. Edited by K.N. Igumnov and Y.I. Mil'shteyn. 250pp. 9 x 12.
22919-X Pa. $5.00

TRISTAN UND ISOLDE, Richard Wagner. Full orchestral score with complete instrumentation. Do not confuse with piano reduction. Commentary by Felix Mottl, great Wagnerian conductor and scholar. Study score. 655pp. 8⅛ x 11.
22915-7 Pa. $10.00

FAVORITE SONGS OF THE NINETIES, ed. Robert Fremont. Full reproduction, including covers, of 88 favorites: Ta-Ra-Ra-Boom-De-Aye, The Band Played On, Bird in a Gilded Cage, Under the Bamboo Tree, After the Ball, etc. 401pp. 9 x 12.
EBE 21536-9 Pa. $6.95

SOUSA'S GREAT MARCHES IN PIANO TRANSCRIPTION: ORIGINAL SHEET MUSIC OF 23 WORKS, John Philip Sousa. Selected by Lester S. Levy. Playing edition includes: The Stars and Stripes Forever, The Thunderer, The Gladiator, King Cotton, Washington Post, much more. 24 illustrations. 111pp. 9 x 12.
USO 23132-1 Pa. $3.50

CLASSIC PIANO RAGS, selected with an introduction by Rudi Blesh. Best ragtime music (1897-1922) by Scott Joplin, James Scott, Joseph F. Lamb, Tom Turpin, 9 others. Printed from best original sheet music, plus covers. 364pp. 9 x 12.
EBE 20469-3 Pa. $6.95

ANALYSIS OF CHINESE CHARACTERS, C.D. Wilder, J.H. Ingram. 1000 most important characters analyzed according to primitives, phonetics, historical development. Traditional method offers mnemonic aid to beginner, intermediate student of Chinese, Japanese. 365pp.
23045-7 Pa. $4.00

MODERN CHINESE: A BASIC COURSE, Faculty of Peking University. Self study, classroom course in modern Mandarin. Records contain phonetics, vocabulary, sentences, lessons. 249 page book contains all recorded text, translations, grammar, vocabulary, exercises. Best course on market. 3 12" 33⅓ monaural records, book, album.
98832-5 Set $12.50

MANUAL OF THE TREES OF NORTH AMERICA, Charles S. Sargent. The basic survey of every native tree and tree-like shrub, 717 species in all. Extremely full descriptions, information on habitat, growth, locales, economics, etc. Necessary to every serious tree lover. Over 100 finding keys. 783 illustrations. Total of 986pp.
20277-1, 20278-X Pa., Two vol. set $8.00

BIRDS OF THE NEW YORK AREA, John Bull. Indispensable guide to more than 400 species within a hundred-mile radius of Manhattan. Information on range, status, breeding, migration, distribution trends, etc. Foreword by Roger Tory Peterson. 17 drawings; maps. 540pp.
23222-0 Pa. $6.00

THE SEA-BEACH AT EBB-TIDE, Augusta Foote Arnold. Identify hundreds of marine plants and animals: algae, seaweeds, squids, crabs, corals, etc. Descriptions cover food, life cycle, size, shape, habitat. Over 600 drawings. 490pp.
21949-6 Pa.$5.00

THE MOTH BOOK, William J. Holland. Identify more than 2,000 moths of North America. General information, precise species descriptions. 623 illustrations plus 48 color plates show almost all species, full size. 1968 edition. Still the basic book. Total of 551pp. 6½ x 9¼.
21948-8 Pa. $6.00

AN INTRODUCTION TO THE REPTILES AND AMPHIBIANS OF THE UNITED STATES, Percy A. Morris. All lizards, crocodiles, turtles, snakes, toads, frogs; life history, identification, habits, suitability as pets, etc. Non-technical, but sound and broad. 130 photos. 253pp.
22982-3 Pa. $3.00

OLD NEW YORK IN EARLY PHOTOGRAPHS, edited by Mary Black. Your only chance to see New York City as it was 1853-1906, through 196 wonderful photographs from N.Y. Historical Society. Great Blizzard, Lincoln's funeral procession, great buildings. 228pp. 9 x 12.
22907-6 Pa. $6.00

THE AMERICAN REVOLUTION, A PICTURE SOURCEBOOK, John Grafton. Wonderful Bicentennial picture source, with 411 illustrations (contemporary and 19th century) showing battles, personalities, maps, events, flags, posters, soldier's life, ships, etc. all captioned and explained. A wonderful browsing book, supplement to other historical reading. 160pp. 9 x 12.
23226-3 Pa. $4.00

PERSONAL NARRATIVE OF A PILGRIMAGE TO AL-MADINAH AND MECCAH, Richard Burton. Great travel classic by remarkably colorful personality. Burton, disguised as a Moroccan, visited sacred shrines of Islam, narrowly escaping death. Wonderful observations of Islamic life, customs, personalities. 47 illustrations. Total of 959pp.
21217-3, 21218-1 Pa., Two vol. set $10.00

INCIDENTS OF TRAVEL IN CENTRAL AMERICA, CHIAPAS, AND YUCATAN, John L. Stephens. Almost single-handed discovery of Maya culture; exploration of ruined cities, monuments, temples; customs of Indians. 115 drawings. 892pp.
22404-X, 22405-8 Pa., Two vol. set $8.00

CONSTRUCTION OF AMERICAN FURNITURE TREASURES, Lester Margon. 344 detail drawings, complete text on constructing exact reproductions of 38 early American masterpieces: Hepplewhite sideboard, Duncan Phyfe drop-leaf table, mantel clock, gate-leg dining table, Pa. German cupboard, more. 38 plates. 54 photographs. 168pp. 8⅜ x 11¼.   23056-2 Pa. $4.00

JEWELRY MAKING AND DESIGN, Augustus F. Rose, Antonio Cirino. Professional secrets revealed in thorough, practical guide: tools, materials, processes; rings, brooches, chains, cast pieces, enamelling, setting stones, etc. Do not confuse with skimpy introductions: beginner can use, professional can learn from it. Over 200 illustrations. 306pp.   21750-7 Pa. $3.00

METALWORK AND ENAMELLING, Herbert Maryon. Generally conceded best all-around book. Countless trade secrets: materials, tools, soldering, filigree, setting, inlay, niello, repoussé, casting, polishing, etc. For beginner or expert. Author was foremost British expert. 330 illustrations. 335pp.   22702-2 Pa. $3.50

WEAVING WITH FOOT-POWER LOOMS, Edward F. Worst. Setting up a loom, beginning to weave, constructing equipment, using dyes, more, plus over 285 drafts of traditional patterns including Colonial and Swedish weaves. More than 200 other figures. For beginning and advanced. 275pp. 8¾ x 6⅜.   23064-3 Pa. $4.00

WEAVING A NAVAJO BLANKET, Gladys A. Reichard. Foremost anthropologist studied under Navajo women, reveals every step in process from wool, dyeing, spinning, setting up loom, designing, weaving. Much history, symbolism. With this book you could make one yourself. 97 illustrations. 222pp.   22992-0 Pa. $3.00

NATURAL DYES AND HOME DYEING, Rita J. Adrosko. Use natural ingredients: bark, flowers, leaves, lichens, insects etc. Over 135 specific recipes from historical sources for cotton, wool, other fabrics. Genuine premodern handicrafts. 12 illustrations. 160pp.   22688-3 Pa. $2.00

THE HAND DECORATION OF FABRICS, Francis J. Kafka. Outstanding, profusely illustrated guide to stenciling, batik, block printing, tie dyeing, freehand painting, silk screen printing, and novelty decoration. 356 illustrations. 198pp. 6 x 9.
21401-X Pa. $3.00

THOMAS NAST: CARTOONS AND ILLUSTRATIONS, with text by Thomas Nast St. Hill. Father of American political cartooning. Cartoons that destroyed Tweed Ring; inflation, free love, church and state; original Republican elephant and Democratic donkey; Santa Claus; more. 117 illustrations. 146pp. 9 x 12.
22983-1 Pa. $4.00
23067-8 Clothbd. $8.50

FREDERIC REMINGTON: 173 DRAWINGS AND ILLUSTRATIONS. Most famous of the Western artists, most responsible for our myths about the American West in its untamed days. Complete reprinting of Drawings of Frederic Remington (1897), plus other selections. 4 additional drawings in color on covers. 140pp. 9 x 12.
20714-5 Pa. $3.95

How to Solve Chess Problems, Kenneth S. Howard. Practical suggestions on problem solving for very beginners. 58 two-move problems, 46 3-movers, 8 4-movers for practice, plus hints. 171pp. 20748-X Pa. $2.00

A Guide to Fairy Chess, Anthony Dickins. 3-D chess, 4-D chess, chess on a cylindrical board, reflecting pieces that bounce off edges, cooperative chess, retrograde chess, maximummers, much more. Most based on work of great Dawson. Full handbook, 100 problems. 66pp. 7⅞ x 10¾. 22687-5 Pa. $2.00

Win at Backgammon, Millard Hopper. Best opening moves, running game, blocking game, back game, tables of odds, etc. Hopper makes the game clear enough for anyone to play, and win. 43 diagrams. 111pp. 22894-0 Pa. $1.50

Bidding a Bridge Hand, Terence Reese. Master player "thinks out loud" the binding of 75 hands that defy point count systems. Organized by bidding problem—no-fit situations, overbidding, underbidding, cueing your defense, etc. 254pp. EBE 22830-4 Pa. $2.50

The Precision Bidding System in Bridge, C.C. Wei, edited by Alan Truscott. Inventor of precision bidding presents average hands and hands from actual play, including games from 1969 Bermuda Bowl where system emerged. 114 exercises. 116pp. 21171-1 Pa. $1.75

Learn Magic, Henry Hay. 20 simple, easy-to-follow lessons on magic for the new magician: illusions, card tricks, silks, sleights of hand, coin manipulations, escapes, and more —all with a minimum amount of equipment. Final chapter explains the great stage illusions. 92 illustrations. 285pp. 21238-6 Pa. $2.95

The New Magician's Manual, Walter B. Gibson. Step-by-step instructions and clear illustrations guide the novice in mastering 36 tricks; much equipment supplied on 16 pages of cut-out materials. 36 additional tricks. 64 illustrations. 159pp. 6⅝ x 10. 23113-5 Pa. $3.00

Professional Magic for Amateurs, Walter B. Gibson. 50 easy, effective tricks used by professionals —cards, string, tumblers, handkerchiefs, mental magic, etc. 63 illustrations. 223pp. 23012-0 Pa. $2.50

Card Manipulations, Jean Hugard. Very rich collection of manipulations; has taught thousands of fine magicians tricks that are really workable, eye-catching. Easily followed, serious work. Over 200 illustrations. 163pp. 20539-8 Pa. $2.00

Abbott's Encyclopedia of Rope Tricks for Magicians, Stewart James. Complete reference book for amateur and professional magicians containing more than 150 tricks involving knots, penetrations, cut and restored rope, etc. 510 illustrations. Reprint of 3rd edition. 400pp. 23206-9 Pa. $3.50

The Secrets of Houdini, J.C. Cannell. Classic study of Houdini's incredible magic, exposing closely-kept professional secrets and revealing, in general terms, the whole art of stage magic. 67 illustrations. 279pp. 22913-0 Pa. $2.50

THE MAGIC MOVING PICTURE BOOK, Bliss, Sands & Co. The pictures in this book move! Volcanoes erupt, a house burns, a serpentine dancer wiggles her way through a number. By using a specially ruled acetate screen provided, you can obtain these and 15 other startling effects. Originally "The Motograph Moving Picture Book." 32pp. 8¼ x 11. 23224-7 Pa. $1.75

STRING FIGURES AND HOW TO MAKE THEM, Caroline F. Jayne. Fullest, clearest instructions on string figures from around world: Eskimo, Navajo, Lapp, Europe, more. Cats cradle, moving spear, lightning, stars. Introduction by A.C. Haddon. 950 illustrations. 407pp. 20152-X Pa. $3.00

PAPER FOLDING FOR BEGINNERS, William D. Murray and Francis J. Rigney. Clearest book on market for making origami sail boats, roosters, frogs that move legs, cups, bonbon boxes. 40 projects. More than 275 illustrations. Photographs. 94pp. 20713-7 Pa. $1.25

INDIAN SIGN LANGUAGE, William Tomkins. Over 525 signs developed by Sioux, Blackfoot, Cheyenne, Arapahoe and other tribes. Written instructions and diagrams: how to make words, construct sentences. Also 290 pictographs of Sioux and Ojibway tribes. 111pp. 6⅛ x 9¼. 22029-X Pa. $1.50

BOOMERANGS: HOW TO MAKE AND THROW THEM, Bernard S. Mason. Easy to make and throw, dozens of designs: cross-stick, pinwheel, boomabird, tumblestick, Australian curved stick boomerang. Complete throwing instructions. All safe. 99pp. 23028-7 Pa. $1.50

25 KITES THAT FLY, Leslie Hunt. Full, easy to follow instructions for kites made from inexpensive materials. Many novelties. Reeling, raising, designing your own. 70 illustrations. 110pp. 22550-X Pa. $1.25

TRICKS AND GAMES ON THE POOL TABLE, Fred Herrmann. 79 tricks and games, some solitaires, some for 2 or more players, some competitive; mystifying shots and throws, unusual carom, tricks involving cork, coins, a hat, more. 77 figures. 95pp. 21814-7 Pa. $1.25

WOODCRAFT AND CAMPING, Bernard S. Mason. How to make a quick emergency shelter, select woods that will burn immediately, make do with limited supplies, etc. Also making many things out of wood, rawhide, bark, at camp. Formerly titled Woodcraft. 295 illustrations. 580pp. 21951-8 Pa. $4.00

AN INTRODUCTION TO CHESS MOVES AND TACTICS SIMPLY EXPLAINED, Leonard Barden. Informal intermediate introduction: reasons for moves, tactics, openings, traps, positional play, endgame. Isolates patterns. 102pp. USO 21210-6 Pa. $1.35

LASKER'S MANUAL OF CHESS, Dr. Emanuel Lasker. Great world champion offers very thorough coverage of all aspects of chess. Combinations, position play, openings, endgame, aesthetics of chess, philosophy of struggle, much more. Filled with analyzed games. 390pp. 20640-8 Pa. $3.50

SLEEPING BEAUTY, illustrated by Arthur Rackham. Perhaps the fullest, most delightful version ever, told by C.S. Evans. Rackham's best work. 49 illustrations. 110pp. 7⅞ x 10¾. 22756-1 Pa. $2.00

THE WONDERFUL WIZARD OF OZ, L. Frank Baum. Facsimile in full color of America's finest children's classic. Introduction by Martin Gardner. 143 illustrations by W.W. Denslow. 267pp. 20691-2 Pa. $2.50

GOOPS AND HOW TO BE THEM, Gelett Burgess. Classic tongue-in-cheek masquerading as etiquette book. 87 verses, 170 cartoons as Goops demonstrate virtues of table manners, neatness, courtesy, more. 88pp. 6½ x 9¼. 22233-0 Pa. $1.50

THE BROWNIES, THEIR BOOK, Palmer Cox. Small as mice, cunning as foxes, exuberant, mischievous, Brownies go to zoo, toy shop, seashore, circus, more. 24 verse adventures. 266 illustrations. 144pp. 6⅝ x 9¼. 21265-3 Pa. $1.75

BILLY WHISKERS: THE AUTOBIOGRAPHY OF A GOAT, Frances Trego Montgomery. Escapades of that rambunctious goat. Favorite from turn of the century America. 24 illustrations. 259pp. 22345-0 Pa. $2.75

THE ROCKET BOOK, Peter Newell. Fritz, janitor's kid, sets off rocket in basement of apartment house; an ingenious hole punched through every page traces course of rocket. 22 duotone drawings, verses. 48pp. 6⅞ x 8⅜. 22044-3 Pa. $1.50

PECK'S BAD BOY AND HIS PA, George W. Peck. Complete double-volume of great American childhood classic. Hennery's ingenious pranks against outraged pomposity of pa and the grocery man. 97 illustrations. Introduction by E.F. Bleiler. 347pp. 20497-9 Pa. $2.50

THE TALE OF PETER RABBIT, Beatrix Potter. The inimitable Peter's terrifying adventure in Mr. McGregor's garden, with all 27 wonderful, full-color Potter illustrations. 55pp. 4¼ x 5½. USO 22827-4 Pa. $1.00

THE TALE OF MRS. TIGGY-WINKLE, Beatrix Potter. Your child will love this story about a very special hedgehog and all 27 wonderful, full-color Potter illustrations. 57pp. 4¼ x 5½. USO 20546-0 Pa. $1.00

THE TALE OF BENJAMIN BUNNY, Beatrix Potter. Peter Rabbit's cousin coaxes him back into Mr. McGregor's garden for a whole new set of ˋdventures. A favorite with children. All 27 full-color illustrations. 59pp. 4¼ x 5½. USO 21102-9 Pa. $1.00

THE MERRY ADVENTURES OF ROBIN HOOD, Howard Pyle. Facsimile of original (1883) edition, finest modern version of English outlaw's adventures. 23 illustrations by Pyle. 296pp. 6½ x 9¼. 22043-5 Pa. $2.75

TWO LITTLE SAVAGES, Ernest Thompson Seton. Adventures of two boys who lived as Indians; explaining Indian ways, woodlore, pioneer methods. 293 illustrations. 286pp. 20985-7 Pa. $3.00

HOUDINI ON MAGIC, Harold Houdini. Edited by Walter Gibson, Morris N. Young. How he escaped; exposés of fake spiritualists; instructions for eye-catching tricks; other fascinating material by and about greatest magician. 155 illustrations. 280pp. 20384-0 Pa. $2.50

HANDBOOK OF THE NUTRITIONAL CONTENTS OF FOOD, U.S. Dept. of Agriculture. Largest, most detailed source of food nutrition information ever prepared. Two mammoth tables: one measuring nutrients in 100 grams of edible portion; the other, in edible portion of 1 pound as purchased. Originally titled Composition of Foods. 190pp. 9 x 12. 21342-0 Pa. $4.00

COMPLETE GUIDE TO HOME CANNING, PRESERVING AND FREEZING, U.S. Dept. of Agriculture. Seven basic manuals with full instructions for jams and jellies; pickles and relishes; canning fruits, vegetables, meat; freezing anything. Really good recipes, exact instructions for optimal results. Save a fortune in food. 156 illustrations. 214pp. 6⅛ x 9¼. 22911-4 Pa. $2.50

THE BREAD TRAY, Louis P. De Gouy. Nearly every bread the cook could buy or make: bread sticks of Italy, fruit breads of Greece, glazed rolls of Vienna, everything from corn pone to croissants. Over 500 recipes altogether. including buns, rolls, muffins, scones, and more. 463pp. 23000-7 Pa. $3.50

CREATIVE HAMBURGER COOKERY, Louis P. De Gouy. 182 unusual recipes for casseroles, meat loaves and hamburgers that turn inexpensive ground meat into memorable main dishes: Arizona chili burgers, burger tamale pie, burger stew, burger corn loaf, burger wine loaf, and more. 120pp. 23001-5 Pa. $1.75

LONG ISLAND SEAFOOD COOKBOOK, J. George Frederick and Jean Joyce. Probably the best American seafood cookbook. Hundreds of recipes. 40 gourmet sauces, 123 recipes using oysters alone! All varieties of fish and seafood amply represented. 324pp. 22677-8 Pa. $3.00

THE EPICUREAN: A COMPLETE TREATISE OF ANALYTICAL AND PRACTICAL STUDIES IN THE CULINARY ART, Charles Ranhofer. Great modern classic. 3,500 recipes from master chef of Delmonico's, turn-of-the-century America's best restaurant. Also explained, many techniques known only to professional chefs. 775 illustrations. 1183pp. 6⅝ x 10. 22680-8 Clothbd. $17.50

THE AMERICAN WINE COOK BOOK, Ted Hatch. Over 700 recipes: old favorites livened up with wine plus many more: Czech fish soup, quince soup, sauce Perigueux, shrimp shortcake, filets Stroganoff, cordon bleu goulash, jambonneau, wine fruit cake, more. 314pp. 22796-0 Pa. $2.50

DELICIOUS VEGETARIAN COOKING, Ivan Baker. Close to 500 delicious and varied recipes: soups, main course dishes (pea, bean, lentil, cheese, vegetable, pasta, and egg dishes), savories, stews, whole-wheat breads and cakes, more. 168pp. USO 22834-7 Pa. $1.75

COOKIES FROM MANY LANDS, Josephine Perry. Crullers, oatmeal cookies, chaux au chocolate, English tea cakes, mandel kuchen, Sacher torte, Danish puff pastry, Swedish cookies — a mouth-watering collection of 223 recipes. 157pp.
22832-0 Pa. $2.00

ROSE RECIPES, Eleanour S. Rohde. How to make sauces, jellies, tarts, salads, potpourris, sweet bags, pomanders, perfumes from garden roses; all exact recipes. Century old favorites. 95pp.
22957-2 Pa. $1.25

"OSCAR" OF THE WALDORF'S COOKBOOK, Oscar Tschirky. Famous American chef reveals 3455 recipes that made Waldorf great; cream of French, German, American cooking, in all categories. Full instructions, easy home use. 1896 edition. 907pp. 6⅝ x 9⅜.
20790-0 Clothbd. $15.00

JAMS AND JELLIES, May Byron. Over 500 old-time recipes for delicious jams, jellies, marmalades, preserves, and many other items. Probably the largest jam and jelly book in print. Originally titled May Byron's Jam Book. 276pp.
USO 23130-5 Pa. $3.00

MUSHROOM RECIPES, André L. Simon. 110 recipes for everyday and special cooking. Champignons à la grecque, sole bonne femme, chicken liver croustades, more; 9 basic sauces, 13 ways of cooking mushrooms. 54pp.
USO 20913-X Pa. $1.25

FAVORITE SWEDISH RECIPES, edited by Sam Widenfelt. Prepared in Sweden, offers wonderful, clearly explained Swedish dishes: appetizers, meats, pastry and cookies, other categories. Suitable for American kitchen. 90 photos. 157pp.
23156-9 Pa. $2.00

THE BUCKEYE COOKBOOK, Buckeye Publishing Company. Over 1,000 easy-to-follow, traditional recipes from the American Midwest: bread (100 recipes alone), meat, game, jam, candy, cake, ice cream, and many other categories of cooking. 64 illustrations. From 1883 enlarged edition. 416pp.
23218-2 Pa. $4.00

TWENTY-TWO AUTHENTIC BANQUETS FROM INDIA, Robert H. Christie. Complete, easy-to-do recipes for almost 200 authentic Indian dishes assembled in 22 banquets. Arranged by region. Selected from Banquets of the Nations. 192pp.
23200-X Pa. $2.50